Pugs

by Liz Palika

ALPHA

A member of Penguin Group (USA) Inc.

ALPHA BOOKS

Published by the Penguin Group

Penguin Group (USA) Inc., 375 Hudson Street, New York, New York 10014, U.S.A.

Penguin Group (Canada), 10 Alcorn Avenue, Toronto, Ontario, Canada M4V 3B2 (a division of Pearson Penguin Canada Inc.)

Penguin Books Ltd, 80 Strand, London WC2R 0RL, England

Penguin Ireland, 25 St Stephen's Green, Dublin 2, Ireland (a division of Penguin Books Ltd)

Penguin Group (Australia), 250 Camberwell Road, Camberwell, Victoria 3124, Australia (a division of Pearson Australia Group Pty Ltd)

Penguin Books India Pvt Ltd, 11 Community Centre, Panchsheel Park, New Delhi—110 017, India

Penguin Group (NZ), cnr Airborne and Rosedale Roads, Albany, Auckland 1310, New Zealand (a division of Pearson New Zealand Ltd)

Penguin Books (South Africa) (Pty) Ltd, 24 Sturdee Avenue, Rosebank, Johannesburg 2196, South Africa

Penguin Books Ltd, Registered Offices: 80 Strand, London WC2R 0RL, England

Copyright © 2005 by Liz Palika

International Standard Book Number: 1-59257-337-1
Library of Congress Catalog Card Number: 2004115922

07   06   05   8   7   6   5   4   3   2   1

Interpretation of the printing code: The rightmost number of the first series of numbers is the year of the book's printing; the rightmost number of the second series of numbers is the number of the book's printing. For example, a printing code of 05-1 shows that the first printing occurred in 2005.

Printed in the United States of America

Most Alpha books are available at special quantity discounts for bulk purchases for sales promotions, premiums, fund-raising, or educational use. Special books, or book excerpts, can also be created to fit specific needs.

For details, write: Special Markets, Alpha Books, 375 Hudson Street, New York, NY 10014.

Publisher: *Marie Butler-Knight*
Product Manager: *Phil Kitchel*
Senior Managing Editor: *Jennifer Chisholm*
Senior Acquisitions Editor: *Mike Sanders*
Development Editor: *Christy Wagner*
Production Editor: *Janette Lynn*

Copy Editor: *Cari Luna*
Cartoonist: *Shannon Wheeler*
Cover/Book Designer: *Trina Wurst*
Indexer: *Angela Bess*
Layout: *Ayanna Lacey*
Proofreading: *Mary Hunt*

Unless otherwise noted, all photographs by Sheri Wachtstetter.

Contents at a Glance

Appendixes

Contents

Foreword

The Pug ... what a lovable, sweet-natured, funny little dog. Small? Yes, to be sure. However, small in the sense that a fireplug is small. Although classified as a toy breed by the American Kennel Club (AKC), the Pug is the largest of the toys. This means a Pug can be hugged, played with, and squeezed (within reason, of course!) without fear of breaking. A Pug is truly a "people" dog. Your Pug will want to be with you every minute of every day; asleep on your foot as you sit on the couch, in your lap as you enjoy the evening news, and nestled in the bend of your leg at night as you sleep. If you make 20 trips down the hallway every day, there'll be a Pug at your heels for all 20 trips. In short, Pugs were bred to be companion dogs, and in that, they excel.

Pugs do not require a lot of exercise; however, it's fine to take your Pug on walks in the morning and evening. The key term here is *walks*. Pugs are not meant to run along after a bicycle. With their short nasal passages, Pugs do not have unlimited breathing capability.

As with any pet, Pugs can be susceptible to certain health problems. Some Pugs can be allergic to fleas; however, your veterinarian can help you prevent this problem. Pugs can also have eye problems. Pugs also often snore. There's nothing wrong with them; they just snore. If this bothers you, don't get a Pug.

In my work with rescue Pugs, I am often asked, "Are Pugs good with children?" More to the point would be, "Are children good with Pugs?" Pugs are one of the most loving, good-natured, patient dogs in the world. In fact, it is the Pugs who suffer more at the hands of loving but misguided children. Pugs tend to take the abuse until they are hurt and even then rarely bite or display any temper.

Many Pugs are turned in to rescue groups because the Pug cannot be housetrained. Please be patient and spend the time with your Pug to acquaint him with your expectations regarding feeding times and place, socialization with other family members and pets, and housetraining. Pugs want to please their people; you can help him by being consistent in your commands and in the times you take him outside. If you take the time to establish a routine and stick to it, your dog will reward you by being much more consistent himself in his toiletry habits.

Most important, please understand that choosing a pet—any pet—is a lifetime commitment. For better or for worse, in sickness or in health, you are your pet's source of care, food, health, and love. Please honor that commitment for the lifetime of your precious pet.

Best wishes to you and the new Pug in your life.

Pug hugs,

Barbara McNair, president, Pug Rescue of San Diego County

Introduction

The Complete Idiot's Guide to Pugs is not like most of the other dog breed books you've read. Most breed books are written by judges, exhibitors, and fanciers of that particular breed and will tell you in no uncertain terms how wonderful their breed is. You'll see photos of winning show dogs, awesome stud dogs, and famous breeders who made the breed so popular. Well, this book isn't like those books at all.

I am not a Pug breeder, nor am I a conformation judge specializing in Pugs. Rather, I am a dog obedience instructor. I see more than 700 dogs and their owners each year in my classes, with two to three dozen of those being Pugs. Many of those new dog owners did a lot of research before adding a new dog to their family, yet at some point they discovered their new dog isn't quite what their research showed it to be. They really didn't know as much about their breed as they thought.

This book will take a realistic look at Pugs, their good points, and some of their less-than-good points. I'll talk about what makes a Pug a wonderful companion and a few of those things that can make living with a Pug a little more of a challenge. You might find a Pug sounds like exactly the right dog for you, or you might decide that a Pug isn't quite what you're looking for. If that's the case, great! It's much better to find out before you bring home a new dog and everyone gets attached to him.

Once you decide to add a Pug to your family, Part 2 will help you get ready for your new family member. You'll find out how to Pug-proof your house and yard and what landscaping plants might be dangerous. You'll also learn why household rules are important and how to begin establishing them. I'll also talk about housetraining—one of the breed's challenges—and how to go about housetraining your dog simply yet effectively.

Part 3 will show you how to keep your Pug clean and well groomed and how to care for him. Part 4 will take you through the training process and also answer a number of questions about training, Pug antics, and canine behavior.

This book was written for people who are thinking of adding a Pug to their family or people who already have one and would like to understand their dog a little better. This book might not highlight the Pugs who have won numerous dog shows, but it is all about Pugs!

Who Am I?

As a dog obedience instructor with more than 25 years of experience, I have answered numerous questions from Pug owners who simply don't understand their dog. They don't understand why their Pug does what he does and are usually frustrated, often angry, and always at their wits end. Their Pugs usually pull on the leash, often have housetraining challenges, and are always having a great time at their owner's expense. But Pugs don't have to be so obnoxious; in fact, they should never be this bad!

I teach dog obedience classes because I love dogs. My husband and I have been married 30 years this year, and we have had dogs the entire time. In fact, we met through our dogs—mine was trained and his wasn't! We enjoy a variety of activities with our dogs, from showing them in obedience to camping with them in the high Sierra Nevada Mountains. Our dogs are our companions, friends, confidants, and protectors.

However, when a dog becomes obnoxious, he's no longer a friend. When dog owners understand why a dog does what he does, they can then either learn to change the behavior or learn to live with it. When dog owners don't understand their dogs, the levels of frustration and anger can escalate until the dog is no longer a treasured member of the family and is discarded. My goal is to be sure dog owners realize they have the means to ensure their dog is a friend and a companion rather than a pain in the, um, neck!

I have taught all levels of obedience, from puppy classes through advanced levels of training, called utility. I have also taught agility classes and therapy dog training. My primary focus, however, is teaching pet owners how to train their family dogs to be well-behaved members of the family, and I have found this to be very rewarding. When someone enrolls in one of my classes and says, "I took your classes 15 years ago with my first dog. She was a wonderful dog but just passed away. We have a new puppy now and want her to be just as good a dog as our first dog was," I know all my time and efforts are worth it!

Decoding the Text

You don't need to be a expert on dogs (or anything else!) to understand this book. There will be no technical gibberish of any kind, and any words I feel need to be defined will be.

You'll find four different kinds of sidebars throughout the book, each designed to add some additional information to the text.

  Pug Smarts
These tips will help make life with a Pug much easier.

 Watch Out!
Pay attention to these boxes. This information is important.

 Pug Speak
These canine definitions will help you understand the information being discussed in the text.

 Bet You Didn't Know
These boxes contain some more information you might find helpful or amusing.

Special Thanks

This text was reviewed by an expert who double-checked the accuracy of what you'll learn here. I have worked with Beth Adelman on several projects, and she is always helpful, accurate, and knowledgeable. An experienced dog book editor, she is also the former editor of *Dog World* and the *AKC Gazette* magazines. Thanks, Beth!

Thanks, too, to Buddy and Sheri Wachtstetter and their Pug, Gordan. The Wachtstetters took the majority of the wonderful photos you'll see throughout this book. Gordan, bless his heart, posed for several of the photos, especially the grooming and health-care ones, and was incredibly patient throughout the process. Gordan is a certified therapy dog, too, and regularly visits nursing homes, schools, and libraries, spreading Pug cheer.

Trademarks

All terms mentioned in this book that are known to be or are suspected of being trademarks or service marks have been appropriately capitalized. Alpha Books and Penguin Group (USA) Inc. cannot attest to the accuracy of this information. Use of a term in this book should not be regarded as affecting the validity of any trademark or service mark.

Part

Is a Pug Your Perfect Dog?

Pugs are different from other dogs; they have a unique look and a different attitude toward life. Pugs were not bred to herd sheep, guard buildings, or hunt rodents. They were designed to be companions to their people. And don't think Pugs don't know they're special; they do!

In the upcoming chapters, we'll take a look at what makes Pugs so special and unique, including their history, their physical conformation, and their personality. I'll also show you how to find a breeder who can help you choose the right Pug puppy for you or the rescue group that can assist you in adopting an older puppy or an adult Pug.

Owning a Pug Is a Partnership

In This Chapter

- 🏠 Introducing Pugs
- 🏠 Pug popularity—increasing by leaps and bounds
- 🏠 Amazing Pug versatility
- 🏠 Owning a Pug and fun go hand in hand

Pugs are different from other dogs. With their short, stocky build and lack of a muzzle, they don't look quite like most other dogs. Pugs also have a unique attitude toward life: they know they are companion dogs, they know they are well loved, and they know without doubt they are special. Add to that the fact that Pug owners are unlike other dog owners and it's easy to see why Pugs are in a whole different realm of canine reality!

A Pug's Special Characteristics

Every Pug owner you meet will tell you that Pugs are not like other dogs. Granted, they do have a different look, but there are several brachycephalic (flat-faced) breeds, so that's not it entirely. The difference has more to do with their heritage and attitude. Pugs have not been bred for anything except companionship. They are not worried about herding sheep, or when sheep aren't available, herding the kids. Nor are they focused on catching every mouse or tracking the flight of birds overhead. Pugs were not bred for such menial chores, and they know it! Pugs know they're special, and this shows in their attitude.

Small but Sturdy

Pugs are small dogs, usually weighing between 14 and 18 pounds full grown. But don't be fooled by the term *small dog*; Pugs are strong and sturdy. They aren't as delicate as most toy breed dogs, yet they don't take up as much space as a larger breed. Pugs are a nice in-between size; small enough to sit on your lap and cuddle, and still strong and sturdy enough to do what you want to do.

Pugs are great walking companions and will be happy to walk with you every day, rain or shine. Well, some Pugs really do hate the rain (and snow, hail, and other bad weather). But if the weather's not bad, Pugs love to go for walks!

Pugs also like to play games, chase balls, run the agility course, and have fun. They are not long-distance runners, and although they have fun in agility, they are not as fast as some other breeds their size.

A Pug is small but sturdy. Can you keep up?

Oh, That Face!

Pugs have a unique face that Pug owners absolutely love. The short muzzle, round head, and black muzzle markings create a wonderfully appealing expression. Add in the big, dark eyes and the wrinkles on the forehead, and there's no other breed of dog with the same look.

The downside to that face is that it requires some care. The eyes are vulnerable without a protruding muzzle to protect them, and the skin folds need regular cleaning.

But beware! Pugs learn very quickly that people think they're cute and use that to their

Bet You Didn't Know
When Napoleon married Josephine, she brought her treasured Pug, Fortune, with her to her marriage. On their wedding night, when Napoleon approached his new wife's bed, Fortune bit him!

advantage. There isn't a Pug owner alive who hasn't asked her Pug to do something, only to have the dog turn that face toward her with a sad, mournful look and a tilt of the head that says, "Do I really, really have to?"

Social Butterflies

Pugs were bred to be companion dogs thousands of years ago, and they remain companion dogs today. Pugs are housedogs and companions. They should never be expected to stay in the backyard for hours at a time; they need to be with their people.

Pug owners often say they can't take their dog for a walk without someone stopping them along the way to talk about their Pug. Pugs create interest. People want to pet them, ask questions about them, and make comments about the breed's appearance and personality. Jeffrey King, from Carlsbad, California, got his first Pug after his wife passed away. He said, "I can't be lonely with Belle around. Not only is she great company, but when we're out on walks, every woman in sight wants to pet Belle and talk to me!"

The breed's love for people also enables them to be wonderful therapy dogs. Certified therapy dogs visit people in hospitals, nursing homes, schools, and day-care centers. With a good foundation of obedience training, Pugs are natural therapy dogs.

Creatures of Habit

Some dog breeds are flexible in their daily routine; most Pugs are not. Pugs thrive on a routine that stays very much the same from day to day. Breakfast and dinner should arrive at set times, and walks should occur at the same time each day. Bedtime, of course, should also happen when it's supposed to!

Some exceptions are allowed, of course. If a visit to the dog park, or a therapy dog visit, or a training class happens once a week, most Pugs will agree that's okay. But a constantly changing schedule will not make a Pug happy.

Intelligent and Trainable

Pugs are not dumb. They really aren't, although there are rumors to the contrary. Joanne Tilver, of Oklahoma City, Oklahoma, uses an old cliché to describe her Pug Mandy: "Mandy is as dumb as a fox. She may want me to think she's dumb, but she isn't. She can open any sliding glass door in the house and open all the bottom kitchen cupboards. She knows how to get me to play with her and how to weasel her way into running errands with me. Pugs are too smart; they just want you to think they're dumb so you don't catch on." She paused, "I guess that means they're smarter than we are."

Pugs are also incredibly stubborn and determined when they're focused on something. If a Pug is trying to get into a kitchen cupboard, he will work at it and think about it until he gets into that cupboard. Although this stubbornness can hinder learning sometimes (especially if the Pug and owner are thinking about two different things!), it can also help. When Pugs are trying to learn what their owners want them to learn, that determination is a wonderful thing.

Pugs don't always do as well in obedience training as many other breeds. That doesn't mean the breed is not intelligent; it just means that Pugs need some motivation. Pugs want to know what's in it for them. When a Pug's owner or trainer knows how to motivate the dog, that changes things. Many Pugs have done very well in advanced obedience training as well as a variety of dog sports and activities.

Pug owners need to learn to have fun with dog training. If they take it too seriously, the training will not succeed. Pug owners also need to be inventive and creative, because what works for Golden Retrievers and German Shepherds will not necessarily work for Pugs.

Bet You Didn't Know

As of this writing, the only Pug to earn a Utility Dog Excellent degree from the American Kennel Club (AKC) is a black Pug, Ch. Webb's Neu Prize Fighter UDX, owned by Christine Dresser, DVM, of Richfield, Ohio.

Pugs are intelligent and trainable but can be stubborn.

Pugs Snore (and Snort, Grunt, and Fart)!

Pugs are not quiet dogs. They're not normally problem barkers, but they do make a variety of biological noises. They snore, snort, sniffle, grunt, fart, and make a variety of other noises. You always know when a Pug is in the house, even if he's sleeping.

Because of their very short face, pushed-in nose, and convoluted nasal passages, Pugs often breathe through their mouth as much as or more than they do through their nose. When they're sleeping, this mouth breathing turns into snoring, just as it does with people. Pugs also make a variety of other noises when they're breathing. Unfortunately, this unnatural breathing can cause some health problems. (I'll discuss this in more detail in Chapter 12.)

This breed also talks by grunting, growling, woofing, whining, and barking. Many Pug owners firmly believe Pugs think they are people and try to speak as people do.

Pugs also make noise (and smells) from the other end. Not to be gross, but most Pugs fart. They can make noise as they do so (to give you fair warning of what's coming), or they will let go silently and the smell will sneak up on you. Many times this can be lessened with a good-quality diet, but some Pugs just seem to have this tendency, and even changing foods or adding supplements doesn't help.

Pet Professionals Speak

Pug breeders obviously love their breed, as do people who own just one or two. However, pet professionals can give an unbiased view of the breed.

Debra Eldredge, DVM, from Vernon, New York, said, "Most of the Pugs I see are generally healthy. In hot, humid weather, they can be prone to respiratory problems, and many are overweight." Dr. Eldredge added that she also sees a few Pugs with skin problems. She said, "I know many Pugs have some serious health problems, but I've been fortunate in my practice to see very few of those. I like Pugs. My grandmother had one, and she was wonderful. Pugs have the best ears in dogdom—just like velvet!"

Petra Burke, co-owner of Kindred Spirits Dog Training in Vista, California, sees about a dozen Pugs per year in her dog training classes. "Pugs can be a challenge to train because they do have minds of their own. However, when the owner discovers how to get their Pug's attention—with treats, a ball, or a squeaker toy—then training is much, much easier. The biggest problem behavior we see in Pugs is housetraining. Pug puppies can be a challenge to house-train, and many frustrated owners have called us after the carpet is already ruined." Burke continued, "But Pugs can be housetrained. It takes time and patience and persistence on the owner's part, but it can be done."

Janice Cartwright grooms dogs in San Diego, California. "I don't see many Pugs," she says, "probably because they have a short coat and their owners bathe them at home. I do know from the ones I see that Pugs can shed a lot and shed all year round. Actually it's amazing how much these small guys shed." Cartwright added, "I do have a dozen or so who come in regularly to have their nails trimmed." She paused and then said carefully, "Pugs are very strong and very strong willed. It can be really hard to trim their nails when they don't want them trimmed." She said, "I think most Pugs are very nice dogs. I just see the ones who have difficulties with their nails, so I'm not necessarily seeing the nicest Pugs."

Rick Hawes is president of the Foundation for Pet Provided Therapy, an organization that evaluates and certifies therapy dogs for volunteer work. "We have several Pugs in our membership. They have all been wonderful therapy dogs, very well behaved and very empathic with the people they're visiting. We'd love to have five times as many Pugs as we have now!"

Don't Rush In!

Pugs aren't perfect; none of us—human or canine—has achieved that distinction yet. However, before you decide to add a Pug to your family, it's always good to know the pros and the cons of the breed.

The pros:

🏠 Pugs are not all alike. They have a variety of personalities.

🏠 Pugs are intelligent and trainable.

🏠 Pugs love people.

🏠 Pugs are small enough to cuddle yet sturdy.

🏠 Pugs have a unique, funny look and a wonderful expression.

The cons:

🐾 Pugs have a mind of their own.

🐾 Pugs can be a challenge to motivate for training, and they can be difficult to housetrain.

🐾 Pugs dislike change, especially a disruption of their schedule.

🐾 Pugs snore, sniffle, sneeze, and make a variety of sometimes-disruptive biological noises.

🐾 Pugs can have some potentially serious health problems.

Pugs are fascinating dogs. If you can take the bad with the good and not let the negative aspects of the breed outweigh the positive ones, a Pug might well be the right breed for you.

Pug Popularity

Throughout their history, Pug popularity has ebbed and flowed. Pug popularity has increased in the past couple decades, however. In 1993, Pugs were ranked as the twenty-eighth most popular breed by the American Kennel Club (AKC), but in just three years, the breed had jumped to number 19 by 1996. By 2003, Pugs were number 12 with 21,340 dogs registered.

Although this increase can be attributed to more people appreciating the wonderful qualities of the breed, the popular media have made the breed itself more recognizable. *Milo and Otis* (White Star Pictures) was one of the first films in recent years to star a Pug (Otis was the Pug). *Men in Black* and especially *Men in Black II*

Bet You Didn't Know

Many experts believe that only one of five puppies eligible to be registered with the AKC actually are registered by their new owners. So the figure of 21,340 Pugs registered with the AKC does not represent the true numbers of Pugs being kept as pets. The numbers are significantly higher.

(Columbia Pictures) made Frank, a Pug, a star, and in the process, made Pugs much more popular. In recent years, Pugs have also been seen in commercials and several television shows, including *Dharma and Greg*.

Popularity has its benefits and problems. Pugs are more recognizable, and professionals (especially veterinarians) are becoming more knowledgeable of the breed's needs. It is also much easier for potential Pug owners to find a puppy today than it was several decades ago. More important, this increasing popularity and the accessibility of the Internet has made researching the breed, as well as its advantages and disadvantages, much easier.

Popularity has its downsides, too, though. One of the biggest problems plaguing any breed that has been highlighted in the media is that potential owners (or new owners) sometimes subconsciously expect the dog to act like the character in the movies or on television. This invariably leads to disappointment. All Pugs are not Otis or Frank, and even the dogs who played those parts do not act like those characters at home.

Pugs have been popular for thousands of years and retain that popularity today with people of all ages.

Popularity also increases the numbers of dogs being bred, and that isn't always good, either. People often want to take advantage of the latest fad, and many puppies will be produced to meet the demand for Otises and Franks. Pugs can have some potentially seriously health problems, and breeders must be well informed of these prior to producing puppies.

Overbreeding has also increased the need for Pug rescue. Rescue groups take in Pugs who cannot remain in their original homes and find new, hopefully permanent, homes for them.

Pugs Can Do Anything (Almost!)

Pugs are toy dogs, but they're not fragile. They are sturdy, well-built dogs who can do just about anything other dogs can do. Granted, they have short legs and sometimes need to catch their breath, but if you want to participate in some dog sports and activities, you can do a lot with a Pug.

Pugs in Conformation

The ultimate goal of conformation dog shows is to choose the best dogs available for breeding so only the best are bred, to continue to improve the breed. But showing dogs is also a sport that thousands of people enjoy every weekend all over the country, and the world.

In conformation dog shows, dogs compete against the same breed, then the Best of Breeds compete against the same class (toys, working class, etc.), then the winner of each class goes on to compete in Best of Show.

Bet You Didn't Know

More conformation dog shows are being seen on television lately. The Westminster Dog Show, held in Madison Square Garden in New York City, is probably one of the most well-known dog shows in the world.

Bet You Didn't Know

In 2003, 214 Pugs were awarded their breed championship through the AKC.

Pugs compete in all breed dog shows and at Pug-only specialty shows. If you want to watch some Pugs competing, you can find a listing of upcoming dog shows at the AKC website, www.akc.org.

Pugs in Obedience

Obedience dog trials originated to highlight well-trained dogs. In the beginning, these events were just for exhibition. Today, thousands of people train their dogs at various levels of training, from the basic heel, sit, down, and stay, through very advanced training, including scent discrimination and hand signals, to earn a variety of obedience degrees.

Bet You Didn't Know

In 2003, Pugs earned 22 Companion Dog degrees (the beginner level of obedience competition), 5 Companion Dog Excellent degrees (intermediate level), and 2 Utility Dog degrees (advanced level)—all through the AKC.

Many Pugs have competed in obedience quite successfully, although some others have had less-than-successful careers, thanks to the breed's stubborn streak. However, obedience competition is certainly possible for any Pug as long as the Pug's owner learns how to motivate her Pug and has patience, persistence, and a sense of humor.

Pugs in Agility

Agility is a fast-paced, athletic sport that's just as much fun for the spectators as it is for the participants. Agility began as a combination of a Grand Prix jumping course for horses and a military dog obstacle course. Today, dogs dash through tunnels, jump over a variety of jumps, climb obstacles, all the while racing against the clock.

Although Pugs are not as athletic as Border Collies or Shetland Sheepdogs and do not have the work ethic of Australian Shepherds or German Shepherds, they can still have great fun with agility— some very successfully. And agility can be competitive or just for fun and exercise.

Bet You Didn't Know

In 2003, Pugs earned 45 agility titles from the AKC, ranging from the basic levels of competition all the way through more advanced jumping titles.

Therapy Pugs

Therapy dogs are those dogs who have been trained, evaluated, and certified to visit people who need some attention, love, and affection. Therapy dogs often visit people in hospitals, retirement homes, and nursing facilities. They also visit day-care centers, schools, and libraries.

As dogs bred to be companions to people, Pugs make awesome therapy dogs. The hardest part is often the basic obedience training that must be completed prior to therapy dog certification. But once certified, Pugs have served admirably as loving, empathic therapy dogs.

 Bet You Didn't Know

Gordan, a Pug owned by Buddy and Sheri Wachstetter of Vista, California, is certified through the Foundation for Pet Provided Therapy. He visited several schools in eastern San Diego after the devastating wildfires of October 2003. He made the kids smile and laugh and allowed those who needed to cry something warm to hug as they cried.

Pugs in Other Dog Sports and Activities

Pugs can compete in other dog sports and activities, although their skills and athletic limitations might hinder them. Let's take a look at a few of the dog sports and activities Pugs can participate in:

🐾 **Carting.** Dogs have pulled wagons, sleds, and travois long before horses were domesticated, but this was never a job for Pugs. Pugs are strong for their size, though, and can pull tiny wagons as long as the wagon is very lightweight, there is little or no load, and the Pug is physically fit.

🐾 **Flyball.** This sport requires a dog to jump four hurdles, bounce on a wall that releases a tennis ball, grab the tennis ball, and return over the four hurdles. It's a fast-paced, exciting relay race. The height of the hurdles is determined by the height of the dogs on each team, so most teams like to have at least one small dog. Although many small breeds are faster, Pugs have participated in flyball quite capably and had great fun doing so.

🐾 **Freestyle.** Freestyle is a combination of obedience competition and dancing. The dog and owner usually have matching outfits or costumes and dance together to music. The dog's dance steps might be built around obedience commands or actual dance steps. This is great fun for dogs and owners, and Pugs do well in it—especially because Pugs love to show off in front of a crowd!

No one should ever assume that a Pug can't do something; the breed has been surprising people for thousands of years. Pugs are strong, sturdy little dogs who love to do things with their owner. If you approach dog sports and activities with a sense of fun (rather than seriousness), as long as the Pug is physically capable of doing it, he will do everything he can.

Pug People Have Fun!

Just as Pugs are unique little dogs, the people who own them are special, too. It seems it takes a different type of person to really enjoy Pugs (and I speak from experience!).

Clubs and Organizations

Dog owners like to hang out together. Whether it's people who own the same breed of dog or people who participate together in dog sports, people have been forming dog clubs and organizations for many years. People who own Pugs do the same thing.

The Pug Dog Club in Britain (www.pugdogclub.org.uk) was formed in 1881. The club's goal is to promote and support Pugs in all aspects of the breed's life with people. The club's Pug handbook is very educational, and the website's gallery of British champions is wonderful.

In the United States, the Pug Dog Club of America (PDCA; www.pugs.org) was founded in 1931. The first Pug dog show took place in 1937 in Madison, New Jersey. The club's website has some important health information pertaining to the breed, as well as links to many sites, including breeders and rescue groups.

Other Pug clubs have formed in locations all over the United States and the world. (Several are listed in Appendix B.) Most groups invite all Pug owners to join, not just those who show their Pugs in dog shows, but pet owners, too. The groups can be a great source of information about the breed, especially if you need help. The meetings and get-togethers are a great way to meet other people who are enthused about the breed and who can talk nonstop about anything Pugs. Older members are also usually very helpful for new members who might want to get started in conformation competition.

There are also a variety of other clubs formed to promote other dog activities and sports. There are clubs for dog owners interested in obedience, agility, flyball, freestyle, and therapy dogs. These clubs are usually for dog owners with all breeds of dogs (not just Pugs). Clubs such as these can help you learn all about the sport and can guide you and your dog as you begin training and competing.

Pug people love their dogs and enjoy sharing them.

Pug Parties

On Saturday, May 1, 2004, more than 535 Pugs showed up at the Del Mar Fairgrounds in Del Mar, California, for a Pug party. This particular party is an annual event to benefit Pug Rescue, an organization that takes in Pugs who can no longer remain in their homes and finds them new ones. The goal for the 2004 event was to raise $14,000 for rescue needs, which often includes veterinary care.

At this Pug party, there were games, lots of costumes, and a whole lot of socializing. Pugs played and splashed in shallow kids' pools while their owners introduced themselves to other Pug owners and chatted. Lots of photographs were taken, including Pugs perched on the seat of a Harley-Davidson motorcycle, many dressed in goggles and scarves. There was also lots of Pug stuff for sale—everything from ceramic statues to jewelry and dog toys.

Not all Pug events are as elaborate. Some might be simple picnics where dogs and people can relax and socialize. Other Pug groups get together to walk in their local community's holiday parades. No matter what the reason, Pug people like to get together, share their dogs, and sometimes feel sorry for people who own any other breed of dog.

The Least You Need to Know

- Pugs are small, sturdy, adorable dogs who love people.

- Pugs snore, grunt, and fart—and they can be incredibly stubborn when they want to be.

- Pugs are more than couch potatoes. They can compete in obedience, run an agility course, and serve as awesome therapy dogs.

- Pug people tend to be as friendly, social, enthusiastic, and unique as their dogs.

2

What Makes a Pug a Pug?

In This Chapter

- 🏠 Checking out the breed's Chinese origins
- 🏠 Traveling the world with the Pug
- 🏠 Understanding the breed standard
- 🏠 Using the breed standard

The Pug is a very old breed with a known history going back to China before 400 B.C.E. Some breed experts believe the breed is even older, dating back as far as 1000 B.C.E., but as with so much ancient history, records are no longer available. The history that is known shows us a dog who traveled often, going from China to the far corners of the world. But no matter where the Pug lived, he was always a treasured companion.

Pug History Mysteries

Some dog breeds have a very clear, well-known history. German Shepherds, for example, were originally bred by one man. His name is known, as well as where he lived and worked and why he wanted a new breed of dog. History even names the individual dogs used to create the breed we know today.

Pugs, however, are not that well defined. Pugs are a very ancient breed, and more is unknown than is known. The breed originated before many written records were kept, and even then, some of the records were known to have been destroyed. Luckily, some records as well as artwork have survived, and of course, legends abound.

The Chinese Connection

As far as we can tell from ancient records, artwork, and legends, the Pug originated in China. The earliest known Pugs were kept by Buddhist monks in Tibet, but the breed quickly became the favorites of the nobility. However, all was not wonderful, because we know that somewhere around 200 to 225 B.C.E., records concerning the dogs were destroyed. Emperor Chin Shih Huang, who unified the then very divided China during that era, was an arrogant man with strong opinions. He was also known as a hands-on leader. For some reason, at some point during his reign, the early history of the breed that became today's Pugs disappeared.

Bet You Didn't Know

Pugs were, at different times during their history, known as the *Sichuan Pai* dog (*Sichuan* refers to the province where the breed was found and *Pai* to the breed's shortened face and short legs). Later, they were known as *Lo-Sze* (for a town in Sichuan).

For most of their history in China, Pugs were treasured dogs. By law, they could only be owned by nobility or by Buddhist monks. However, because they were held in such high regard, they were also used as pawns in international relations. In 732 C.E., China gave a Pug to Japan as a gift to cement diplomatic relations. The Japanese became infatuated with this dog, and it became the first of many given to Japanese diplomats.

During the Ming dynasty (1368–1644), Pugs and other dogs lost much favor with the Chinese royalty. (Cats became the pet of choice!) But by the late seventeenth century, Pugs had regained much of their previous popularity. In the late nineteenth century, the Dowager Empress Tzu Hsi was a big fan of Pugs and kept many dogs in the palace, feeding them exotic foods and assigning servants whose sole job was looking after the dogs.

The world began trading regularly with China in the early sixteenth century, and these funny-looking yet exotic Chinese dogs were highly treasured the world over. Traders from all over Europe, including Portugal, Spain, Holland, and Great Britain, were known to have traded for Pugs and brought them home.

All the Way to Europe

Holland became the Pug's first stronghold in Europe. William the Silent, of the House of Orange (1533–1584), had a Pug named Pompey. During a Spanish attempt to gain control over Holland, Spanish troops attacked a camp where William the Silent was sleeping. Pompey, who went everywhere with his master, alerted the camp and his master of the approaching troops, thereby averting a tragedy. After that heroism, Pompey (and Pugs in general) became the honored pets of the Dutch nobility. When William became King of England in 1688, he took a great many Pugs with him. Even in death, William had his Pugs nearby; a Pug is carved at the foot of the statue of William that stands at his tomb.

After William's death, Pugs remained a favorite of the British royalty for generations. Queen Victoria and her son Edward VII kept Pugs as well as detailed records of the dogs and their progeny. Later, in the 1900s, when Edward VIII abdicated his throne to marry his love, Wallis Simpson, they took refuge in France and brought their Pugs with them.

At times during their history, black Pugs were scorned. Today, they are gaining in popularity.

Old artwork from Europe also shows the breed's popularity. William Hogwarth painted *The Painter and His Pug* in 1745. The dog portrayed is very definitely a Pug, although the nose is slightly longer than we see in today's Pugs, and the legs are longer, too. Hogwarth's critics were quick to point out the resemblance between the dog and his owner, both of whom had high, round foreheads and pronounced jowls. Hogwarth's Pugs were named Pugg and Trump.

Bet You Didn't Know

The original meaning of the name *Pug* is not known, nor is it known why it's applied to this breed. In Latin, *pug* means "clenched fist" (as in a fighter—a pugilist). In old England, a *pug* was a term of endearment for a slightly naughty child.

More Recent History

Pugs were probably first introduced to the United States in the late 1800s. We don't know for sure because of the lack of written records; many dogs were brought into the country as pets, were never shown at a dog shows, and if bred, were bred as pets and companions. However, several Pug enthusiasts imported Pugs from Great Britain in the late 1800s and early 1900s, and these dogs became the foundation of the breed in the United States. The AKC recognized the breed in 1885, and the Pug Dog Club of America (PDCA) was established in 1931.

The breed lost contact with its Chinese heritage in 1949 when the Communist Party came into power in China. This was a time of great upheaval in China. People were starving all over the country, and the Communist Party leaders considered it a waste of food to feed pet dogs. All pet dogs were ordered destroyed, and dogs whose lineage went back thousands of years were killed. Luckily, enough Pugs had been exported from China previously that the breed continued.

Breed Standards

Every country's kennel club that recognizes Pugs has a breed *standard* that is the official written description of the breed in that particular country. A breed standard provides guidelines for breeders wanting to breed better dogs; they can compare potential breeding stock against the standard to choose the best dogs for breeding. Conformation dog show judges compare the dogs competing at each dog show to each other and to the standard to choose the dog who best conforms to the breed standard on that day.

Pug Speak

A breed **standard** is the official written description of an ideal dog of that breed. It is what keeps a Pug looking like a Pug and not a Greyhound!

The AKC breed standard was approved on October 8, 1991, and became effective on November 28, 1991. The Kennel Club of

Pug Smarts

For a complete copy of the AKC Pug breed standard, go to www.akc.org. For a copy of the British Pug breed standard, go to www.the-kennel-club.org.uk. The Australian breed standard can be found at www.ozpugs.com, and the New Zealand breed standard is at www.nzkc.org.nz.

Great Britain (or Kennel Club UK) approved Pugs for Champion status in 1886, although the Pug Dog Club of England was recognized in 1883. In the past decades, many other countries have adopted standards for Pugs. Here are summaries and explanations of the most important aspects of several different breed standards. Try to visualize each description and fit the pieces together like a canine jigsaw puzzle.

General Appearance

Pugs should appear square, *cobby*, compact, and well-muscled. A good Pug is symmetrical, with each side of his body a mirror image of the other side. Pugs are compact (*multum in parvo*), as if a lot of dog is shoved into a small package.

Pug Speak

Cobby means "short-bodied and compact." *Multum in parvo* means "much in little," although Pug owners have adapted it as their motto: "A lot of dog in a small space."

Pugs should not be leggy, lean, or long-bodied. Pugs, both males and females, should weigh between 14 and 18 pounds. Males should look masculine (heavier boned, with a slightly broader head), and females should have a very feminine (but not fragile) appearance.

Characteristics and Temperament

Pugs are charming, easygoing, and very appealing to people of all ages, but especially to children. Pugs should have a stable temperament. They can be protective without being aggressive and playful

without being too hyperactive. Pugs are dignified yet not so dignified that they can't act silly at times. The Pug's even temperament
and simple joy in life makes him an ideal companion dog.

Although the Pug's physical appearance is the breed's trademark,
that appearance would be nothing without the breed's known personality. Pugs are popular because of their charming personality and
as such, Pugs should not be fearful or aggressive.

Head and Muzzle

A Pug's head is *brachycephalic* and should be round and slightly flattened at the top, although with no indentations in the skull. This
round skull demonstrates *neoteny*, and retains a "baby" look quite
often seen in toy breeds.

The *muzzle* is short, blunt, quite square in appearance, and has a
wide underjaw. The Pug's bite is slightly *undershot*, with the lower
jaw protruding slightly. The Australian standard stresses that the
teeth should not show when the mouth is closed, and the tongue
should not hang out of the mouth. This is not a truly functional
mouth; a Pug would have a difficult time as a hunter. However, due
to Pugs' companion status through history, they have not had to
hunt, so a hunter's jaw or mouth is not necessary.

Pug Speak _____
Brachycephalic refers to the skull shape and length. A brachycephalic skull has a broad base and a very short length
(including a short muzzle). **Neoteny** is the retention of juvenile
features into adulthood. People are often more drawn to an animal who continues to appear babylike. **Muzzle** refers to the part
of the skull from under the eyes forward to the nose, top and
lower jaws, and the supporting bone. When the bite is **undershot,** the lower jaw protrudes slightly so the bottom teeth are
slightly in front of the top teeth.

The skin of the head has large, deep wrinkles on the forehead, around and between the eyes, and around the muzzle. These wrinkles are a vital part of the Pug's history; the wrinkles on the forehead form the Chinese character for "prince."

A Pug's face and expression are two of the breed's most appealing features.

Eyes

The Pug's eyes are very large, very round, and globular. The eyes should also be very dark and bold. Eyes such as these continue the neoteny appeal.

When a Pug's relaxed, his eyes should convey a soft expression, showing affection. When he's excited, though, the eyes should convey boldness and passion.

Many breeds of dogs have eyes that are inset more than the Pug's eyes are. When inset, the eyes are more protected by the bones of the skull—important to a working dog. A Border Collie, for example, herding sheep through tall grass or brush, needs protection for his eyes. The Pug, however, shows his status as a companion rather than a working dog with vulnerable, protruding eyes.

Ears

The Pug's ears are small, thin, silky, and soft. Both the British KC and AKC Pug breed standards refer to the breed's ears as "black velvet." Two types of ear shapes are accepted—the *rose* ear and the *button* ear. With the rose ear, the ear flap is folded over toward the back to reveal the burr inside the base of the ear. With the button ear, the ear flap folds forward, covering the inside of the ear.

Neck and Body

The neck is strong and thick, continuing to carry through with the well-muscled, cobby, compact look of the body. The neck should be long enough to carry the head proudly but not so long as to look out of balance.

The body is short and compact. The chest is wide with plenty of room for the lungs and heart. The back is short and level, keeping the body looking square.

The front legs are straight, powerful, and set well under the body, not out to the side. The *hindquarters* should be in balance with the *forequarters*. The feet are medium size with black nails.

Despite the Pug's companion status (he's not a working dog), he should still be strong with the appearance of being perfectly capable of working. His body should not appear fragile, soft, or weak.

Pug Speak

Forequarters refers to the area on the Pug from his shoulders all the way down his front legs to his feet. **Hindquarters** refers to the hips and pelvis all the way down the rear legs to the feet.

Tail

The Pug's tail is an interesting little thing and just calls out for your fingers to play with it! The tail is called a curled tail or a twisted tail. The ideal tail is curled as tightly as possible over the hip. A tail that curls twice is preferred over a tail that only curls once.

Coat and Colors

The Pug's coat is short, fine, glossy, and invites petting. The hair is soft, not hard, bristly, or wooly.

Three coat colors are accepted by the AKC and New Zealand standards: silver, apricot-fawn, and black. The *markings* should be defined and black. Acceptable markings are the mask or muzzle, a diamond in the middle of the forehead, cheek moles, and a trace (or stripe) that follows the spine from the head to the tail.

Pug Speak

Markings are areas of the Pug's coat that are a different color than the base coat, often a contrasting color.

The British KC and Australian standards accept four colors: silver, apricot (a warm fawn), fawn, and black. The acceptable markings are the same as those in the AKC standard.

Movement

Pugs move naturally at a trot, and when trotting, they should appear confident and self-assured, even bold. When viewed from the front, the front legs should be straight with no weakness at the *pasterns*, and the feet should hit the ground straight and square. When viewed from the rear, the hind legs should also be square, although the hips will roll slightly.

Pug Speak

The **pastern** is roughly comparable to a human's wrist.

Using the Standard

Breed standards were written to keep a breed true to type and form. Although many of today's Pugs are pets and will never see the inside of a show ring, the standard still has applications. Even pet Pugs should be strong and able to play hard. A Pug who conforms closely to the standard is more likely to be a well-put-together Pug and less apt to have wrist, elbow, or hip problems. And breeders (professional, hobby, or first-time breeders) should always take the standard into consideration prior to breeding any Pugs.

The Least You Need to Know

- Pugs were bred to be companion dogs and continue to serve that purpose today.
- Breed standards (AKC, KC, and others) describe the ideal Pug.
- Today's Pug is a confidant, affectionate, and bold small dog.
- The Pug is a lap dog but is also strong, well muscled, and able to play.

Chapter 3

Finding the Pug for You

In This Chapter

- 🏠 Getting your Pug from a breeder
- 🏠 What is Pug rescue?
- 🏠 Adopting a Pug from a shelter
- 🏠 Picking the perfect Pug for you

Finding the right Pug for you isn't as easy as simply taking home the first available dog. That particular dog might have a personality that clashes with yours, or worse yet, he might not like your kids. Adding a dog to your family means adding another family member, so it's important to find just the right dog who will mesh with your family as if he's always been there.

Finding a Reputable Breeder

The ideal place to find your new family member is with a reputable breeder. What makes a breeder "reputable"? A reputable breeder …

- 🏠 Knows the breed standard well and can explain it you, using a dog as a physical guide.

- 🏠 Chooses her breeding stock carefully, breeding only the best.

- 🏠 Will not breed dogs with health problems and will use medical tests to eliminate any dogs who could pass along inherited defects.

- 🏠 Keeps herself informed and is continually trying to improve her dogs.

- 🏠 Knows Pugs are not the right breed for everyone and tries to weed out those people who would be disappointed with a Pug.

- 🏠 Tries to find the right home for each puppy and will ask prospective owners many questions before allowing them to buy a puppy from her.

- 🏠 Will take back any Pug from her breeding program if that dog does not work out in its first home.

- 🏠 Will listen to the people who have bought dogs from her so that she can learn the good points (and bad) concerning her dogs.

Finding That Special Breeder

There are many ways to find that special Pug who's just right for you. I found my dog, Care Bear, by talking to someone who had a puppy from a breeder. They were thrilled with their dog, Sunny, and raved about how well the breeder had treated them. I got the breeder's name and number and contacted her myself; Care Bear was the result!

If you see a nice Pug walking with his owner, stop and talk. Ask where the Pug came from, and ask the Pug's owner if she would go back to the same breeder for her next Pug. If she is thrilled with her dog and the dog is healthy, she probably will. However, if there were problems, or if the dog is not healthy, the Pug's owner might decide to look elsewhere for their next dog.

You can also find a breeder by going to a local dog show or two and talk to the people showing their Pugs. Wait until the Pugs have finished showing before you approach them. If you try to talk to anyone before they compete, they will be nervous and potentially rude because of the upcoming competition. But after the competition is over, people relax and are usually happy to stop and talk.

The Pug Dog Club and the AKC also maintain breeder referral lists. You can find the AKC's breeder referral list at www.akc.org/breeds/breederinfo/breeder_search.cfm and the Pug Club at www.pugs.org/indexbreeder.htm. Be aware that these lists are not endorsements of quality; they are simply lists of people who breed Pugs.

What Is a Backyard Breeder?

A *backyard breeder* is someone who breeds dogs but doesn't do as much research or have as much information about the breed as

is needed to do it well. Sometimes people have bought a good-quality dog (or simply paid a lot of money for a dog) and want to earn back their investment. Others think breeding dogs is a good way to make money. No matter what their reason to breed, the dogs produced by backyard breeders are not normally as nice as those produced by a reputable breeder.

Pug Speak
A **backyard breeder** is someone who breeds her dog (or dogs) but doesn't have the knowledge about her breed that a reputable breeder has worked so hard to learn.

Some dogs produced by backyard breeders have been very nice, but many others have not. Most backyard breeders do not have the understanding of canine genetics to produce truly nice dogs generation after generation, and the majority are not willing to spend the money on health tests to be sure their dogs are not passing along hereditary defects.

Someone who wishes to begin breeding Pugs should ask for help from a reputable breeder. If a seasoned, knowledgeable breeder will mentor her, she can learn what she needs to do to improve the quality of her dogs. At that point, she will no longer be referred to as a backyard breeder.

What Is a Puppy Mill?

A *puppy mill* is a breeder who produces puppies as a commodity. This breeder looks upon puppies as a means to make money and is not concerned about adhering to the breed standard or increasing the quality of her dogs. Often the puppy mill is a farm, with dogs kept in small cages. Sometimes a puppy mill is a family home with way too many dogs for the premises.

Pug Speak

A **puppy mill** is a commercial enterprise that produces puppies in large numbers. Dogs are usually kept in cages, receive little to no individual socialization, and no health screenings are done with the breeding stock.

Pug Smarts

To learn more about puppy mills (and to see some photos of Pugs rescued from puppy mills) go to www.michiganpugrescue.com.

In most puppy mills, because profit is a motive, the female dogs are bred each time they come into season and the puppies are taken from their mothers too soon. Pet stores that sell puppies want the puppies by the time they are 8 to 10 weeks old, so the puppies are taken from their mothers at 5 to 6 weeks old. This can cause health problems as some of these puppies fail to thrive. In addition, many puppies taken from their mothers too early develop behavior problems later in life because they missed the nurturing guidance momma dogs provide.

Questions to Ask a Breeder

When you find a breeder or two you would feel comfortable doing business with, ask her some questions. She will be expecting your questions—and would be surprised and probably disappointed if you didn't ask—so don't be shy about calling her.

Here are some things to ask a potential breeder:

- **How long have you been breeding?** Some experience is always better than none, of course, but many years of experience is not always the best, either. Some "old timers" get stuck in a rut and neglect the necessary continuing education. The breeder's answer to this question will have to be balanced with the answers to the following questions as well.

- **Do you show your dogs?** Even if the breeder doesn't show her dogs every weekend, she should at least show her breeding stock prior to retiring them to the whelping box. By showing her dogs at conformation dog shows, the breeder will get someone else's opinion as to the quality of her dogs. If a *bitch* or *dog* she plans to breed does poorly when shown, the breeder should rethink her plans to breed those particular dogs.

Pug Speak
A **bitch** is dog-speak for a female canine. A **dog** is a male canine. To make things more confusing, **dog** or **dogs,** is also appropriate when referring to one or multiple members of the species as a whole.

- **Do you belong to any dog organizations?** Membership in the national and local Pug clubs can help breeders keep up on Pug-related issues, especially new advances in health care.

- **What kind of health problems do you screen your dogs for?** If she says her dogs don't have any health problems, cross this breeder off your list. Unfortunately, Pugs can and do have some health issues, and it's important that breeders don't ignore them. The breeder should be up front with you and discuss these issues in detail. Obviously, she shouldn't be repeatedly breeding dogs with health problems, either.

🏠 **What kind of guarantee do you offer with your dogs?** Is the dog guaranteed to be free of hereditary defects? Or if the dog does develop something, what does the breeder offer to do about it? Although it's very difficult to guarantee that a dog will not develop a problem later in life, this is very important to you.

Watch Out!
The breeder should not take offense when you ask questions about her dogs or her breeding program. If she does, try another breeder.

🏠 **Can I see some of your dogs?** The answer must be yes, even if the breeder has no puppies at the moment. Seeing several of her dogs will give you a good idea of what her breeding program produces. It will also give you a chance to sit down and talk some more.

When You Visit a Breeder

When you find a breeder you like, make an appointment to visit her at a time convenient for both of you. When you visit for the first time, look for a few things:

🏠 **Are the dogs bright-eyed, alert, and friendly?** Pugs are people dogs, and although they'll bark when someone comes to the door, they should settle down as you come in. They should be curious about you and come up to be petted.

🏠 **Do the dogs appear to be healthy?** Older dogs might be gray muzzled, stiff, and have opaque eyes, but younger dogs should be healthy, with clean eyes and healthy skin.

🏠 **Does the breeder call each dog by name, and do the dogs respond?** Sometimes breeders accumulate too many dogs and, therefore, the dogs don't get the individual attention they need. The breeder should know each dog by name, and each dog should respond to his or her name.

🏠 **Is her house, dog yard, and kennel clean?** The dogs in the house should be housetrained. If you go out to the yard or kennel, you should see that feces have been picked up and urine washed down.

If the breeder has puppies, she should be able to show you the registration papers for that litter as well as the parents. Her paperwork must be in order or you won't be able to register your puppy. The breeder should also show you the pedigree for those puppies, as well as a copy of her sales contract. Be sure you read the contract completely. Ask questions if there are points you don't understand.

Watch Out!
Registration papers from the AKC or any other registry are not an assurance of quality. They simply mean the parents were themselves registered.

A responsible breeder will want to be sure you're the right person (and family) for her puppy.

Questions to Expect from a Breeder

Just as you will ask questions of the breeder, she will ask questions of you. Reputable breeders are protective of their puppies; she'll want to be sure you can provide the best home possible for one of her puppies.

Expect some questions such as these from a breeder:

🏠 **Have you owned a dog before? If so, did that dog live out his life with you?** The breeder wants to know that you are committed to caring for a dog, including her puppy, should she sell one to you.

🏠 **Have you owned a Pug before?** Pug breeders know, more than anyone else, that Pugs are different from other breeds of dog. People who have owned Golden Retrievers or German Shepherds might not realize how different Pugs are. If you haven't owned a Pug before, the breeder might ask you how much research you've done on the breed.

🏠 **Is your backyard securely fenced?** Sometimes Pugs can be too curious for their own good, and if your yard is not fenced, or the fence is not secure, the Pug might decide to go exploring.

🏠 **Have your kids been raised around dogs?** Pugs are great with children and make wonderful family dogs, but the breeder will want to be sure your kids won't be cruel to the dog. She might ask you to bring your kids with you to her place for a visit. If she does ask this, it's because she wants to see how your children behave around dogs.

The breeder might ask you a variety of other questions, too. Don't be offended, and just answer the questions as truthfully and completely as possible. After all, you and the breeder are talking about adding a new member to your family; this is an important decision. You should take comfort in that the fact by asking you questions, the breeder is demonstrating that she cares about the future of her puppies.

You should be comfortable bringing home a puppy from the breeder.

Taking a Look at Pug Rescue

Each year, millions of purebred dogs are given up by their owners for a variety of reasons. Sometimes the owner passes away or is transferred overseas, or a child becomes allergic to the pet. The owner may have simply chosen the wrong pet for the family. Whatever the reason, purebred rescue groups take in these dogs from their owners or from shelters, and find new, hopefully permanent, homes for the dogs.

Although puppies are not usually available from rescue, the ages of rescued Pugs vary from young adults to the very old. Sometimes a dog is given up because it has health problems the family either doesn't want to deal with or can't afford to do. If this is the case, the Pug will probably be

Bet You Didn't Know

Pugs often end up in rescue for horrible excuses. Some have not been properly housetrained, and others are given up because they shed!

from 9 months to 2 years old, sometimes older. Once in a while, rescue takes in an old dog who was turned out of the family because the family got a new puppy.

The Pug Dog Club of America (PDCA) is actively involved with rescue, and many local clubs and groups have formed regional rescue groups. Most rescue groups have the Pugs examined by a veterinarian, spayed or neutered, vaccinated if needed, and microchipped for identification.

You won't be able to get as much information about a dog in rescue as you would be able to get from a breeder. Very few dogs in rescue come with their registration papers, so the dog's ancestry will be unknown. But you should be able to find out whether the dog is housetrained, and whether or not the dog is good with kids.

> **Pug Smarts**
>
> Find information on Pug rescue at www.pugs. org; click on "Rescue: Pugs for adoption." Or do an Internet search for a rescue group in your area. On a search engine (such as Google, www. google.com) search for Pugs + rescue + your city or county.

You can find a Pug rescue group in your area by contacting the PDCA, or if there is a Pug club local to your area, ask there, too. You can also check with your local shelter, humane society, or animal control. They usually keep a list of purebred rescue groups. Your veterinarian might also know of a Pug rescue group.

Pug rescue groups will ask you to fill out an application before you even look at any dogs. This might seem strange; after all, when car shopping, you find a car first and then fill out the financial paperwork. It doesn't work that way with rescue, though. The group will first want to find out if you're qualified to adopt one of their dogs.

The rescue group will then contact you for a face-to-face interview, usually in your home. They will want to see you and your family, how your children behave, and whether or not your home and yard appear to be safe for a dog.

When you are approved for adopting a Pug, you will be notified when one is available and invited to meet the dog. If you and the dog seem to like each other, you can then apply to adopt this particular dog. You can also decide to look at a few more dogs if this one doesn't seem to fit.

After the adoption, the rescue group might do one or two follow-up visits to be sure everything is going okay for you and the dog. Rescue groups don't want to see their dogs back in rescue again and will do everything they can to make the adoption work.

You can usually find adult dogs from Pug rescue.

Other Ways to Find a Pug

Many people don't like to buy from a breeder; some blame breeders for the huge numbers of dogs *euthanized* at shelters every year. These people would prefer to save a dog's life by adopting a dog

Pug Speak _____

Euthanasia is a fancy name for saying that a dog is being killed, usually by lethal injection or gas.

who would otherwise be euthanized. Other people prefer to get a dog directly from its first owner so they can learn more about the dog. All these reasons are very personal; there are many different ways to find the right dog for you.

Shelter Adoptions

Dogs end up in local shelters, animal control facilities, or humane societies for a variety of reasons. Some might be been abandoned, and others were turned loose to fend for themselves. Sometimes dog owners have unrealistic expectations, and when the dog can't live up to those expectations, he is turned in to the local shelter.

Adopting a dog from a shelter can be a wonderful thing—after all, you are saving a dog's life who might otherwise be put to sleep. However, shelter adoptions also carry some risk. You won't know this Pug's health history or ancestry. You won't know whether the dog has any behavior problems, whether or not he's been socialized, or even whether he's housetrained or not.

You can ask the shelter staff some questions, though:

- Is the Pug clean in his run?
- Does he appear to be shy around people, or is he eager to greet everyone who comes to his run?
- Does he walk nicely on the leash?
- Does he appear to understand any of the basic obedience commands?
- Was the Pug turned in by his owner, or was he a stray?
- If he was turned in, what information did his previous owners give about him?

In many states, privacy laws prevent the shelters from giving out too many details about the previous owner, but often the shelter staff can give you some information. Sometimes it's just a matter of how you word your questions. Find out as much as you can before you decide to bring home a dog from the shelter. And be sure you are ready to deal with the unknown, whatever it might be!

Private Party Adoptions

There are times when even a very well-loved pet needs a new home. Sometimes a Pug owner simply cannot keep the dog anymore. A military family might be transferred overseas or an elderly owner might have to go to a nursing home.

In these situations, don't get caught up in the emotions of the moment. You're still looking for the right Pug for your family, and this one might or might not be the right dog for you. Ask many of the same questions you would ask a breeder. After all, you're still making the same decision.

Spend some time with the dog before you decide. Play with him; take him for a walk; and check his eyes, teeth, and toenails. Discover what his personality is like, and pay attention to any behavior problems you notice. Be sure this is (or isn't) the right Pug for you before you agree to take him home (or walk away).

Pet Stores

Reputable breeders don't sell their puppies to pet stores. Reputable breeders want to know who is buying their puppies and want to do the screening themselves. Therefore, the puppies in pet stores often come from backyard breeders—or worse yet, puppy mills.

Choosing the Right Dog for You

Every Pug has his or her own personality, but Pugs have less of a variety in temperament than do some other breeds. Some Pugs are sillier than others, while others are more dignified. Some are more easily trained than others, and a few are very stubborn. It's important that you choose the Pug whose personality will mesh nicely with yours with as little discord as possible.

Your Own Personality

Before you can chose a Pug whose personality will complement yours, take a look at yourself. If you choose a Pug whose temperament is the opposite of yours, the conflict could be horrible and your Pug could be one of those looking for a new home. Be honest about yourself when you think of your personality.

If you are …

- **Extroverted, outgoing, boisterous, and exuberant:** Choose the boldest Pug puppy in the litter. You two will rule the world.

- **Easygoing, calm, and tough to rile:** Choose a Pug who is calm but not bold. An extroverted, bold Pug would take advantage of you.

- **Introverted, quiet, and shy:** Choose the quietest Pug available but not a shy one. If you're both shy, you will reinforce the trait in your Pug. Instead, choose a Pug who is quiet and calm but also a touch outgoing. This dog will bring you out of your shell.

By choosing a Pug whose personality will complement yours (rather than clash), you decrease the potential for problems later. In addition, the two of you will have much more fun together!

Boys or Girls?

Both male and female Pugs can be great friends and companions, but each sex does have some specific characteristics. Female Pugs usually bond well with male owners, and male Pugs bond more closely with female owners.

Good pets do not need to have those adult sexual hormones, so females should be spayed and males should be neutered. Neutered males are usually very affectionate and bond closely to their owners. Spayed females are also good companions but can be a touch bossy.

Males can be leg-lifters and might try to mark their territory (inside and out). This can be controlled with some training and supervision. Females sometimes get a little snippy with other female dogs, but again, training is a big help.

Bet You Didn't Know

If you already have a dog at home, bring home a Pug of the opposite sex. There will be fewer disagreements when you keep a spayed female and a neutered male than when you keep two dogs of the same sex.

Puppy or Adult?

Most people assume that a new canine addition to the family should be a puppy, but that might not be the right choice for you.

Puppies are cute and appealing and bond well to people. But puppies are also very time-consuming and require a great deal of effort. It takes 2 years before a Pug is considered mentally grown up and trustworthy in the house unsupervised. Although Pug puppies are not nearly as destructive as many other breeds, they can still get into trouble.

Newly adopted adult Pugs bond well to new owners, although sometimes it takes 2 to 3 months before they really feel comfortable in their new home. Adult Pugs might or might not have some behavior problems, including housetraining issues, depending on their previous owner's training efforts.

Take a good look at what you're doing now, your normal routine at home and at work, your after-work activities, and your family. Decide where and how a Pug would fit into your life and then decide whether a puppy or an adult would be better.

Listen to Your Heart

Choosing the right dog for you can be very difficult. You have so much to think about and so much to discuss with your family. A totally emotional decision is rarely the right one (no matter how cute he is, don't get that Pug in the pet store window!), yet a totally logical decision isn't right, either. You do need to have an emotional attachment to this Pug, yet you need to be somewhat logical and think about your decision. When your brain tells you it's right, let your heart guide you.

My youngest dog was not a planned decision. I was at a dog event when his breeder walked up to me and placed an 8-week-old puppy in my arms. She said, "I know you loved his grandmother. Well, she has passed away, and this puppy is from the last litter of her daughter. Do you want him?" How could I say no to a puppy who was licking my face? Especially one who was the grandson of a dog I absolutely loved?

In this case I knew the breeder and I knew the puppy's ancestors so I didn't have to do any research. However, because I wasn't planning on getting a puppy at that time, it was a purely emotional decision. Of course, I took him home. As I write these words, he's curled up under my desk.

The Least You Need to Know

- A reputable breeder will expect you to ask questions, so go ahead and ask. She will also ask you questions.

- Adopting a Pug from a rescue group can be a rewarding experience.

- Adopting a Pug from a shelter might save his life, but you won't know much if anything about him, so be careful.

- Don't bring home the first Pug who's available; choose the right Pug for you.

Part  2

There's a Pug Puppy in the House!

Pug puppies are so adorable! Their cute little round heads with the soft folds and wrinkles and their stocky bodies and soft coats make them irresistible. But this appeal can get you (and a Pug puppy) into trouble. To prevent any future problems, let's get you both started on the right foot.

Before you bring home your new Pug, be sure you're ready for him. You need to Pug-proof your house and yard so he'll be safe. You'll also need to go shopping for him.

You can begin teaching your Pug puppy some basic household rules as soon as he comes home—and that includes housetraining. Pugs can be tough to housetrain, but it can be done.

Puppies are fascinating creatures, especially Pug puppies, and this is a time for learning and growing. So keep reading!

Chapter 4

Prior Planning for Pugs Is Everything!

In This Chapter

- 🏠 Preparing your house for your new Pug
- 🏠 Making your yard safe for your Pug
- 🏠 Getting help from pet professionals
- 🏠 Shopping for your Pug

You probably fell in love with your new Pug the moment you met him at the breeder's home or at a rescue function; after all, that face is so cute. It's amazing how that cute face will change your life and alter it forever in ways you can't yet imagine.

Some of those changes need to begin even before you bring home your new Pug. You'll want to be sure your home is safe for a Pug because they can get into trouble, especially a curious and active Pug puppy. You will also need to check your yard and fence so your Pug will be secure when he goes outside.

Pet professionals, including a veterinarian, a trainer, and yes, even a groomer, can help you with your Pug over the years to come, so you'll need to touch base with them. And last, but certainly not least, you will want to go shopping for Pug supplies.

Pug-Proofing Your House

Pugs are not nearly as destructive as many other breeds are known for being, but Pug puppies can still wreck havoc with telephone cords, television remote controls, and a nice leather wallet. Pug puppies don't chew to be malicious; they're just puppies looking for something fun. When you're a puppy and can exercise your jaws by chewing on something—and you can tear off pieces as you chew— that's great fun!

You can prevent much of the destruction puppies can cause by picking up things and putting them away. Be sure any children in your house put away their toys and close their bedroom doors. Everyone in the household should be responsible for keeping their clothes off the floor and putting away their shoes, slippers, and dirty socks. Knickknacks, books, magazines, and the remote controls should be kept out of the puppy's reach. Never assume one of your personal items doesn't look appealing to a puppy; puppies don't choose the stuff to chew by eye appeal. Many times the item is chosen because it smells good (like you) and because it feels good in your puppy's mouth. Other times, the puppy might just feel like chewing whatever's closest to him.

Watch Out!

Be especially vigilant when puppies are teething (between 4 and 5 months of age). They will be frantic to chew nearly anything.

Some things puppies often chew on include the following:

- 🏠 Television and electronics remote controls
- 🏠 Telephone and electrical cords

- 🐾 Cell phones
- 🐾 Shoes, socks, slippers, and sandals
- 🐾 Food, dishes, cups, and utensils
- 🐾 Children's toys
- 🐾 Books and magazines

Your Pug puppy probably won't limit his jaw-exercising to just this list. Look around your home from your Pug's perspective and remove anything in his path you don't want gnawed on.

Dangerous Stuff

Our homes are full of dangerous things, and your new Pug will have no idea what's dangerous and what isn't. Anything interesting will be sniffed, pawed at, chewed on, and sometimes even swallowed. It's up to you to protect your Pug from things that can hurt him.

Some potentially dangerous things commonly found in and around our homes include the following:

- 🐾 Medicines and medicine containers, vitamins, and supplements
- 🐾 Cigarettes, cigars, pipes, and pipe tobacco
- 🐾 Pens, pencils, felt-tip markers, and craft and sewing supplies
- 🐾 Household cleaners, including oven cleaners, as well as laundry products
- 🐾 Bath products, colognes and perfumes, shampoos and conditioners, and some makeup items, including nail polish removers

Pug Smarts

If you think your Pug might have swallowed something potentially poisonous, call the National Poison Control Hotline at 1-800-222-1222, or the ASPCA Animal Poison Control at 1-888-426-4435.

Keeping your Pug safe means he'll be around longer for you to love and for him to love you. Our homes are full of dangerous things, so it's up to us to be sure everything is put away in a safe place where the Pug can't reach it.

Limiting Your Pug's Freedom

One of the easiest ways to help protect your Pug is to limit his freedom. You can use baby gates to confine him to one room at a time, preferably the room you're in so you can watch him. When you can't supervise him, put him in his crate (I'll talk more about crates later in this chapter), or put him in a child's playpen or an exercise pen. An exercise pen works much like a child's playpen; it's a small portable fence that can be set up anywhere you need it and will confine the Pug and keep him out of trouble.

Pug puppies are quite small and very curious. They can get into tiny places (like beside and behind the refrigerator). More than one Pug puppy owner has had to pull out the refrigerator or washing machine to rescue a stuck Pug! When you've got a Pug puppy at home, you need to think small and look for those places where the puppy might get into trouble and then restrict the puppy's access to those places.

When you limit your Pug's freedom until he's grown and learned the household rules, you are both keeping him safe and preventing him from learning bad habits.

Pug-Proofing Your Yard

You will need to Pug-proof your yard just as you did your house. Be sure the gardening tools are put away after each use and gardening supplies are stored out of reach. The kids should put away their toys when they're through playing, and the pool chemicals need to be stashed somewhere safe.

Look at your yard from a Pug's point of view (especially his height). Can he chew on the backyard light cords? If he can reach them, he might. Is there a gap under the deck your Pug puppy can fit underneath? Is that a danger to him if he crawls in? There are many things in the backyard that could be dangerous; you need to find them before your Pug does.

Inspect the Fence

Pugs are curious creatures. If there's a hole in the fence, your Pug will try to get through just to see what's on the other side. He's not trying to escape or even necessarily go anywhere; he just wants to explore.

Inspect your fence thoroughly. Fix any gaps or holes in the fence. If your fence has gaps, you might even want to staple or affix hardware cloth (wire fencing) on the inside of your fence from tight to the ground to about three feet high.

Check for holes under the fence, too. Pugs are not normally problem diggers, but they have been known to dig under a fence. The hardware cloth can help here, too, by blocking some of those gaps. You can also fill in any holes under the fence with hard packed dirt, gravel, or stones.

 Bet You Didn't Know

If your yard is not as secure as it should be, or if you feel the yard has too many dangers, build your Pug a dog run. A fenced area 12 feet long by 4 feet wide is plenty big enough to give your Pug some room to stretch his legs.

Is your yard safe for your new Pug puppy?

Dangerous Plants

Many commonly used landscaping plants can be dangerous to your Pug if he chews on them or eats them. Some will make him nauseous, but others are toxic.

The following plants could be dangerous to your Pug:

- Amaryllis
- Avocado (leaves, not fruit)
- Azalea
- Belladonna
- Bird of paradise
- Bottlebrush
- Boxwood
- Buttercup
- Calla lily
- Common privet
- Crocus
- Daffodil
- Dieffenbachia
- Dogwood
- English ivy
- Foxglove

- 🐾 Hemlock
- 🐾 Horse chestnut
- 🐾 Hyacinth
- 🐾 Iris
- 🐾 Jasmine
- 🐾 Lily of the valley
- 🐾 Milkweed
- 🐾 Morning glory

- 🐾 Mushrooms
- 🐾 Oleander
- 🐾 Pennyroyal
- 🐾 Poison oak, ivy, and sumac
- 🐾 Rhododendron
- 🐾 Sweet pea
- 🐾 Tulip
- 🐾 Yew

If you have any questions about the plants in your yard, check with your local horticulturist or poison control center. Before you bring home your puppy and allow him out into the yard, be sure none of these or any other dangerous plants are in your yard.

Dangers from the Sky

One danger to Pugs many people forget about is birds of prey. These birds live by catching small animals. Their normal prey, depending on the species of bird, might be mice, rats, rabbits, squirrels, or even reptiles, including lizards and snakes. Birds of prey are an integral part of our natural ecosystem and do much to control pests.

However, many birds of prey will not hesitate to take small dogs, too. A Pug puppy is tiny enough that many birds of prey, including most hawks, could grab one if the chance arose. Even adult Pugs could be in danger if eagles are in your area.

Watch Out!

Your yard isn't the only place to be aware of birds of prey. Whenever you're outside, walking, picnicking, or especially when hiking in rural areas or camping, keep an eye on the sky—and the other on your Pug.

If you live in an area where birds of prey are common, never allow your Pug outside without your supervision and protection. You might want to build your Pug a covered dog run to prevent birds of prey from getting in. Then, when your Pug goes outside, he should stay in the dog run.

Help from Pet Professionals

As a dog owner, you should never feel like you're alone in caring for your Pug. Many pet professionals are available to help you, no matter what your needs are. Why suffer through anxieties over your Pug's health when a veterinarian can help you? Or why worry about trimming your Pug's nails when a groomer can do it for you—or, better yet, teach you how to trim his nails yourself? Let these professionals help you. That's what they're for!

You can find pet professionals in your area in several different ways, but the most reliable is usually through personal referrals. Ask several different dog owners who they recommend, and if one name keeps popping up, he or she is probably worth getting to know.

Watch Out!

Don't wait for an emergency to find a pet professional. Do your research now, before you need help.

Yellow Page ads are fine, and coupons are okay, but keep in mind that anyone can place an ad. Place more stock in the referrals you get from people you trust. They are speaking with firsthand knowledge.

Your Veterinarian

A veterinarian you trust is vital to help you keep your Pug healthy. You want to work with someone who knows Pugs and who also likes them. Talk to a few Pug owners in your area and find out which veterinarian they work with, or talk to other dog owners in your neighborhood. When you find a couple vets who sound promising, make an appointment to go talk to them before you bring home your puppy. You'll have to pay for the office call, but consider it an investment in your new Pug.

When you go in to the appointment, ask a few questions:

🏠 Do you see many Pugs?

🏠 What health problems do you see in the breed, and how do you normally approach those problems? (In general terms, of course, not specifics.)

Ask the veterinarian about his business policies, too:

🏠 What are your business hours?

🏠 What is the business telephone number?

🏠 What are your emergency procedures? Do you take emergencies, and if so, how can you be contacted? If you don't take emergencies, where should your clients go?

🏠 What are the payment options? Are all payments due in full when performed? Do you accept checks? Credit cards (which ones)? How about debit cards?

When you find a veterinarian you feel comfortable with, set up a client record with him so that when your Pug puppy comes home, you can make an appointment to bring the puppy in for his first exam.

Trainers

You can find a trainer through personal referrals, too. You can also call several local veterinarians' offices and ask who they recommend. After all, the local vets see both well-behaved dogs and rowdy dogs in their offices every day, and they hear which trainers help their clients and which are not as effective. Humane societies and shelters can also refer you to reputable trainers in your area.

When you've found a couple trainers in your area who have come with good referrals, give them a call and ask if you can watch one or two of their classes. There should be no problem with this; most trainers would prefer people come watch before they enroll in training.

As you watch a class, watch the trainer and consider the following:

- Do the students (the human ones and the canine ones) appear to be enjoying the class?

- When the trainer handles one of the student's dogs in class, is the teaching process evident?

- Watch her dog, too. Does her dog appear well behaved? Does her dog appear happy to work?

- Would you be comfortable in this class?

Pet professionals, including a trainer, will be a great help to you throughout your Pug's life.

After class is over, approach the trainer and introduce yourself. Tell her a Pug will be joining your family soon, and ask her a few questions:

- 🐾 Is she familiar with Pugs?

- 🐾 What training challenges does she see with Pugs, and how does she recommend they be handled?

- 🐾 Is she familiar with the house-training problems Pugs can have?

Pug Smarts

Your Pug can begin kindergarten puppy class when he's 10 weeks of age and has had 2 sets of vaccinations. Older Pugs can begin class as soon as they've settled into the household (2 to 3 weeks).

After visiting a couple trainers, decide which you would feel best working with and get a copy of her class schedule so you can begin as soon as your Pug is ready.

Groomers

Many people associate groomers with Poodles or other breeds that regularly get haircuts or need de-matting. Although these dogs do make up most of a groomer's business, a groomer can also be of great help to the Pug owners.

Some Pug owners like to take their Pugs to the groomer's once in a while so a professional can brush out their Pug's shedding coat. Groomers also trim toenails, which can be difficult for many pet owners to do. She will also bathe and brush your Pug and check the anal glands. Groomers can also help control fleas and ticks, if they're present in your area.

A Pug Supply Checklist

Okay, you've checked your house and yard and they're safe and secure for your new Pug. You've found a veterinarian, trainer, and groomer to work with, and you have a Pug all picked out. What else

do you need? How about dog food? Food and water bowls? A leash and collar? You're going to need to go shopping for your new arrival, so let's make a list.

Food and Water Bowls

Pugs have a very short face, so their food and water bowls should be shallow, especially the food bowl. If the bowl is too deep, the Pug will put pressure on the underside of his neck (on the edge of the bowl) trying to reach the food on the bottom of the bowl. A wide, shallow bowl or plate is best for food. The water bowl can be slightly deeper because your Pug will lap the top of the water. Just be sure the water bowl never runs dry!

Ceramic or metal bowls are best. Plastic bowls have a tendency to become play toys.

Dog Food

Have some of the food your Pug is used to eating on hand when you bring him home. If you want to change to another brand or type of food, do so gradually over a couple weeks. Changing right away will give your Pug a tummy ache and diarrhea. (I'll talk more about canine nutrition in Chapter 10.)

Bet You Didn't Know

Take 2 to 3 weeks to completely change your Pug's food. The first week, give your Pug ¼ of the new food and ¾ of the old food. By the end of the first week and beginning of the second week, feed ½ of the old food and ½ of the new food. By the end of the second week, feed ¾ of the new food and ¼ of the old food. By the middle of the third week, feed 100 percent of the new food.

A Place to Potty and Play

Pugs are curious dogs who often aren't worried or afraid even when they should be. Unfortunately, they can get into trouble.

A dog run can keep your Pug from getting into places where he shouldn't be and into stuff he should leave alone. A secure dog run will also prevent escapes, especially if your fence isn't secure. And as I mentioned earlier in this chapter, a covered dog run could potentially save your Pug's life from a swooping bird of prey.

A Pug doesn't need a large dog run. A 12 feet long by 4 feet wide run should be just fine. What's more important is that it's secure and safe.

A Collar and Leash

Every dog should wear a soft buckle collar that snaps around his neck. If you're bringing home a young puppy, you might want to pick up a cat collar. These smaller collars fit toy breed puppies better than most dog collars. Once your Pug grows some, however, a small dog collar should fit.

A 4-foot leash works well for Pugs. A 6-foot leash is too much to handle. Don't worry about getting a retractable leash right now; we'll talk about those in Chapter 14.

Identification

Your Pug needs an identification tag in case that curious little guy ever somehow gets away from you. Most pet supply stores today (and even many discount or department stores) have an ID engraving machine that engraves tags on the spot. Make a tag for your new puppy so you'll have one waiting when you bring him home. You don't even have to have his name on it right now if you haven't decided on one. All you need is your telephone number. That way, if your puppy gets away from you, someone can call you. Later, you can get a new tag with his name on it.

You can also ask your veterinarian about microchipping your Pug. Your vet can inject a microchip into the skin at the Pug's shoulder. This is a permanent identification and is recommended by most vets, animal control officers, and humane societies.

Puppies can be microchipped at 4 months of age, although many shelters do it even younger. Most veterinarians and all shelters have readers that can scan in the information in the chip. Vets or shelter staff can then check online databases that have your specific contact information (that you provide when you register the chip).

Toys!

Your Pug will need toys. Play and chew toys will help keep him occupied and can help prevent damage to your belongings. Pugs like noisy toys, food dispensing toys, and throw toys. They don't always bring back the toys after you've thrown them, but they do like chasing them!

All Pugs need toys!

Bet You Didn't Know

A Pug can have too many toys. If the Pug has a lot of toys, he will think all the world is his and everything is a toy. Instead, give him just two or three toys at a time and teach him what he's allowed to play with and what's off limits. You can rotate toys, though, to keep him amused.

A Crate

A crate is a wonderful training tool. It is necessary for housetraining, and it helps prevent other problem behaviors as well.

There are three basic types of dog crates: plastic, wire-sided, and soft-sided. Pugs do very well in wire-sided crates because the crates allow good air circulation, especially in hot weather. These are usually collapsible and fold down into a storable size.

The crate should be big enough for your Pug to stand up, turn around, and lie down. Don't get a large crate; bigger is not better. A bigger crate gives the dog room to have a housetraining accident and move away from it. (I'll talk more about using the crate in upcoming chapters.)

Baby Gates and Exercise Pens

Baby gates were designed to keep human babies and toddlers safe, but they work just as well for puppies. As I mentioned earlier, a big part of raising a puppy and keeping him safe is preventing him from getting into trouble. A baby gate will close off rooms, block hallways, and limit the puppy's freedom. Baby gates can be a nuisance to use, but you won't have to use them for more than a year or so, just until your Pug knows the household rules and is mentally grown up.

Exercise pens are portable, foldable fences you can buy at pet stores. They are specifically

Pug Smarts

A great place to pick up baby gates are garage sales. Just wash them well before using them.

Bet You Didn't Know

Exercise pens are also great for when you're traveling with your Pug. Throw one in your car, and when you arrive a friend's house, the campground, or even just a picnic, set up the exercise pen. Your Pug can be safe and secure yet still a part of what's going on.

designed to keep a puppy controlled and safe. They can be set up anywhere, restrict your Pug's freedom, and give him more room than a crate does.

Grooming Supplies

Your new Pug won't need a lot of grooming supplies, especially compared to coated breeds such as Bearded Collies or Poodles, but you will need to buy a few things for your new arrival:

- 🐾 Shampoo and conditioner
- 🐾 Toenail clippers
- 🐾 A soft-bristled brush
- 🐾 Cotton balls and antibacterial wipes for cleaning his wrinkles, his ears, and under his eyes

After you've had your Pug a while, you might need some other grooming supplies, but these basics will get you started.

Cleaning Supplies

Puppies do sometimes make a mess, so be prepared. White vinegar is inexpensive and is one of the best products around for cleaning up after housetraining accidents. You'll also want to have some paper towels, a scrub brush, and some trash bags.

What Else Do You Need?

Don't buy an expensive dog bed right now because puppies tend to chew up their beds. Just use a few old towels you can throw in the washing machine.

You might also want a pooper-scooper for the backyard. Other than that, you're all set. Let's bring home that Pug!

The Least You Need to Know

- Pug-proof your house and yard, looking at both from a small dog's perspective.

- A dog run can help keep your Pug safe while he's outside.

- Find a veterinarian, trainer, and groomer you will be comfortable working with.

- Before you bring home your new puppy, go shopping for the supplies you'll need to welcome home your new dog.

Establishing Household Rules

In This Chapter

- 🏠 Learning to be your Pug's leader
- 🏠 Determining which rules are important for your Pug
- 🏠 Teaching your Pug the household rules
- 🏠 Using rules to prevent problems

Pugs need rules in their lives. Like children, they are more secure when there are known rules, boundaries, and a regular routine. Some Pugs will test those rules, but it's just to see if you will be the leader and enforce the rules. When your Pug pushes the edge, it's as if he's saying, "Oh, good. She's paying attention to me. The rules are still there, and she cares enough about me to react."

When you set guidelines for your Pug, you are also preventing some problem behaviors from starting. When a Pug raids the kitchen trash can and finds some leftover food, the bad behavior rewards itself, and he'll definitely try it again to see if he can find more goodies in the trash can! However, if you limit your Pug's freedom, supervise him, and teach him that the trash cans are off limits, he never starts trash-can raiding.

Your Pug Needs a Leader

When your Pug joins your family, you are essentially becoming a substitute (or adoptive) parent. Although many people don't like to think of themselves as a dog's mother or father, that is basically what you must be. In a natural situation, a wild canine never leaves its family as early as domesticated puppies do; 8- to 10- or even 12-week-old puppies still need a

Pug Speak

The **leader**, just like a parent, is fair, firm, and demands respect.

parent. When you set limits for your Pug and teach him correct social behaviors and household rules, you are teaching him proper behavior as a parent would. You are becoming your Pug's *leader.*

This "leader" concept will help you understand why you need to be your Pug's leader right now rather than his best friend. Most of us get dogs, especially Pugs, because we want a best friend and a companion. Your Pug will be able to be that for you eventually, but not right now. Right now he needs guidance. The friendship will come later.

A good, effective parent always treats the young (human or canine) with respect. Parental guidance is kind and caring yet firm. Guidance is always consistent, and rules are enforced. In turn, the parent demands respect from the young. Your role as your Pug's leader is exactly the same.

Here are some guidelines for the leader/young Pug relationship:

- 🏠 Establish the rules early, and enforce them consistently.

- 🏠 Teach your Pug the basic obedience commands, and practice them regularly. Use these commands to teach him the household rules.

- 🏠 Teach your Pug to respect you; be his leader.

Bet You Didn't Know

You must be your Pug's leader (think: parent) throughout his puppyhood. Later, when he's 2 to 3 years old, you can relax a little and he can become your best friend.

If you try to raise your Pug without assuming the leadership position yourself, what will happen? Young dogs need leadership, and without it, your Pug will flounder. He won't learn the rules that make living with a dog a joy. He might also try to take over the leadership position himself or develop behavior problems, including the following:

- 🏠 Growling when you ask him to get off the bed or sofa.

- 🏠 Growling when you try to groom him or trim his toenails.

- 🏠 Growling or snapping when you come around his food, toys, or treats.

- 🏠 A bossy attitude, which might include growling, snapping, and even biting.

- 🏠 Refusal to follow your directions and requests.

- 🏠 Poor housetraining skills, including leg lifting.

- 🏠 Mounting (humping) behavior from males and females.

Pug Smarts

Pug owners like to spoil their Pugs; after all, that's why they chose this special breed. Unfortunately, a spoiled Pug can be a tyrant. Pugs might be unique, but they are still dogs and need leadership.

You and your Pug need to have mutual respect for each other; otherwise, the relationship won't be fun for either of you.

Be Your Pug's Leader

You can do several things to help your Pug understand you're his leader rather than simply his playmate. His mother wouldn't do these kinds of things necessarily; after all, we aren't dogs and would never fool a Pug into thinking we are. But these things will help your Pug understand your respective places in the family:

- Practice your Pug's obedience skills often, and use them in the house as well as outside in the yard, on walks, and out in public. When you use your Pug's training skills and ask him to follow your directions, you are being his leader. (If your Pug does what he wants and you follow, he is being the leader.)

- You should always go first. Teach your Pug to wait at all doorways and then give your Pug permission to follow you. Not only is this good leadership, but this will also protect him from dashing out the front door and into the street. In addition, when your Pug follows you rather than runs ahead, you will be less likely to trip over him, especially with an armload of groceries or laundry.

- Just as the leader should always go first, the leader should also eat first. Eat your own breakfast or dinner, then feed your Pug. The giver of the food is very important, physically and psychologically, to your dog.

- At least once each day, invite your Pug up on your lap and then roll him over so you can give him a tummy rub. This is a submissive position, and although he will enjoy the tummy rub, it's still teaching him to be submissive to you.

- Never allow your Pug to stand over or above you. Many Pugs will jump to the top of the sofa or chair and stand over your head or shoulder. This is an extremely dominant position.

Don't ever allow it. Instead, pull him down and have him lie down next to you on the chair or even on the floor by your feet.

🐾 Give your Pug permission to do things. When he picks up his toy, give him permission and then praise him, "Get your toy! Good boy!" This is what's called "free" training. Your Pug was going to do it anyway, so take advantage of it.

Encourage everyone in the family, especially the children, to follow these guidelines for developing leadership. The children as well as the adults in the family must be leaders for the dog. Many behavior problems come about because the dog respects the adults in the family but feels dominant over the kids.

If someone in the family feels bad and thinks that the Pug should be babied more, remind them that we all have leaders we need to follow. The kids need to listen to their parents and teachers, and the teachers must listen to the principal. We must obey our bosses at work and the police officers out in public. We all have leaders; it's a fact of life. Pugs need leaders, too.

Make Leadership a Habit

Being your Pug's leader is not just for when you're teaching him when he's a puppy. You must continue to be his leader through his puppyhood on into his adolescence and adulthood. Many of the worst challenges (when your Pug decides whether or not you're really his leader) don't happen when your Pug is a puppy but when he's an *adolescent*, about 7 to 10 months of age. When you make leadership a habit, you can either prevent these challenges or at least lessen their impact.

Pug Speak

Adolescence in dogs occurs between 7 and 10 months of age and is much like it is in human children. At this stage of development, the young dog (or human) is striving for independence.

Most Pugs are mentally grown up by 2 to 3 years of age. Notice I said *mentally;* physical maturity and mental maturity don't necessarily happen at the same time. And although physically immature Pugs can be clumsy and awkward, the mental immaturity is what can cause behavior problems. Maintain your leadership skills until your Pug is mentally mature, well trained, and past the stages of challenging your leadership.

Your Pug Needs Rules

Household rules teach your Pug what is and what is not acceptable behavior. There is less confusion all around when the rules are understood than when they aren't clear. When you have established and routinely enforce the rules, your Pug will know exactly what you expect of him.

Watch Out!

When you establish household rules, be sure everyone in the family understands how important they are, and be sure everyone accepts and enforces them. If only one person in the family disagrees and doesn't enforce the rules—or worse yet, encourages the dog to break the rules—the dog will never be sure what's right. He might behave even worse because he'll be confused.

When you are deciding which rules will work best for your dog and your family, keep in mind what your Pug will grow up to be. For example, do you want to allow him up on the furniture? Pugs are not big dogs, so they are nice to cuddle with while you're relaxing in the evening. However, Pugs do shed, and they shed a lot all year round. Think about the pros and cons before you decide on the household rules. Changing your mind 6 months from now can be very confusing to your dog.

Your rules should also take into account your personal likes and dislikes, your daily routine, and any other desires you might have. Perhaps the dog hair on your sofa and throw pillows would end up bugging you. If so, even if you like cuddling with the dog, keep him off the furniture.

Here are a few basic household rules all dogs should follow:

🏠 Housetraining is obvious; your Pug should never relieve himself in the house.

🏠 Your Pug should never use his teeth on people. Biting of any kind, in play or in anger, is not allowed.

🏠 Begging food from people, especially while people are eating, is a bad habit that often turns into stealing food. Likewise, no people should offer the dog treats from the table.

🏠 Your Pug should not sleep on your bed; he needs a bed of his own. This is especially important during housetraining and adolescence. Your bed is the most important bed in the house and belongs to you, not your dog.

Watch Out!

If your Pug sleeps on the bed and growls at you when you move him or ask him to get off the bed, call a dog trainer or behaviorist right away. This could be a serious behavior problem and could result in your dog biting you.

Here are a few more suggestions you might want to discuss with your family:

🏠 Do you want your Pug up on the furniture?

🏠 Do you want to allow your Pug in the kitchen? A Pug is a small dog who is easy to trip over. If you don't see him when you have a hot pan in your hand, it could be disastrous.

🏠 Do you care if your Pug jumps up on you? Big dogs can do a lot of damage jumping up on people, but Pugs are not very big. They can ruin pantyhose, though, and get pantlegs muddy.

Do you want to restrict certain parts of the house? You might want to keep the Pug out of the kids' rooms so he won't get into their stuff. You might want to keep him out of your sewing or craft room because you leave things around in that room you don't want him to get into.

What else is important to you? Think about it, and decide what would make life with a dog easier.

Do you want your Pug on the furniture? Decide now, as you begin setting new rules.

Establishing guidelines as soon as your Pug joins your household will help prevent problem behaviors from getting started. It's much easier to prevent problems and teach the new rules than it is to try to correct problem behaviors later, especially once those behaviors have turned into bad habits.

Pug Smarts

When you and your family have decided on the rules you want your Pug to follow, write down the rules and the commands you'll use to enforce each rule, such as "No begging!" so everyone is using the same language. Also list some quick guidelines on how to handle each situation. Post the rules in a prominent location such as on the refrigerator or the bathroom door where everyone will see it several times each day.

Too Much Freedom

Too much freedom is detrimental to your Pug, plus it's not natural for a dog to have total freedom. Even a wild canine has limits and boundaries. A wolf hunts within his own territory; if he strays beyond those boundaries, he might be attacked and even killed.

Young dogs, especially those under 3 years of age, have very little self-control. Self-control must be learned, and it can be learned, but it also comes with mental maturity. When you allow your dog to have too much freedom too soon and there is no self-control to restrain it, your Pug will likely develop behavior problems.

Bet You Didn't Know

If you give your Pug too much freedom too soon and he gets into trouble, it's your fault, not his. You made the mistake. Your Pug needs guidance from you so he can learn what behavior is right and what is wrong.

A Pug under 3 years of age should have very little freedom. He needs to be kept in the room with you, close to you, with the hallway blocked by a baby gate or exercise pen. If you can't supervise him, he needs to be in his crate, exercise pen, or outside in a safe place such as a dog run.

If the dog is not supervised and raids the trash can, chews on your shoes, relieves himself in the kid's bedroom, or tears up the toilet paper in the bathroom, it's your fault. Yelling at him, hitting him, or otherwise punishing him will not work. These methods will teach your Pug to fear you, but they won't stop these behaviors.

Watch Out!

If your Pug is getting into a lot of trouble (chewing, relieving himself in the wrong places, and other destructive acts), you are probably giving him too much freedom.

Limit freedom outside the house, too. I never allow my dogs to run free off leash outside my fenced yard until they are 3 years old and until their training is good enough that I know they'll come when I call, every time I call. If the dog isn't that reliable, he isn't allowed off leash. It only takes one time for the dog to not respond to be hit by a car, get in a dog fight, or run away. It's much safer to keep your dog on leash unless he's in a fenced yard.

Teaching your Pug the rules early can prevent problem behaviors later.

The Teaching Process

Later, in Part 4, I'll go into the training process in great detail, but to conclude this chapter, let's take a quick look at how you can begin teaching your Pug the household rules.

Restricting your Pug's freedom is the first step, obviously, and you will want to continue doing this until your Pug is mentally and physically grown up.

Keeping your house and yard Pug-proofed is the next step in training your Pug. Don't leave your good leather shoes in the middle of the floor; put them away in your closet where your Pug can't gnaw on them. If things are left out, your Pug is left unsupervised, and something gets chewed, it's not the dog's fault.

However, if you're supervising the dog and he picks up something he shouldn't (such as your leather shoes), here's what to do:

- Take away what he shouldn't have, without turning it into a game of tug-of-war.
- Tell him, "No!" sharply as you take it away.
- Wait a second or two for the correction to sink in and then hand him one of his toys.
- When he takes the toy from you, praise him, saying "Good boy!" in a happy tone of voice.

If he picks up the right thing (his toy, not your shoe) on his own, praise him immediately and enthusiastically, saying "Yeah! Good choice! What a smart dog!"

You can use the same type of teaching for other behaviors. For example, if he wants up on the furniture and you decide you want to keep him off …

- Always praise him when he stays off the furniture. If he walks up to you for petting and puts his head on your leg but doesn't jump up, praise him.
- When he tries to jump up, or begins to climb up, stop him, saying "No! Off the furniture!" and push him down.
- Praise him when all four paws are back on the floor.
- Give him a comfortable spot of his own near where you normally sit. After all, he wants to be near you, and he deserves to be comfy, too. Praise him when he uses this spot on his own.

Use this same type of learning process for teaching all the household rules you want your Pug to learn. It's not hard for you or your Pug. In fact, the hardest thing for most Pug owners is being consistent.

The Least You Need to Know

- You must be your Pug's leader, fair, firm, and loving.

- Household rules give your Pug boundaries and security in knowing what is acceptable behavior.

- Establish rules that will work for you, your family, and your household, then be sure everyone enforces them consistently.

- To prevent problem behaviors or danger to your Pug, limit his freedom until he's mentally and physically grown up.

Chapter 6

Housetraining Your Pug

In This Chapter

🏠 Housetraining your Pug: challenging but doable

🏠 Introducing the crate

🏠 Teaching your Pug where to relieve himself

🏠 Being patience and consistent

According to Pug rescue groups, more Pugs are given up by their owners because of poor housetraining habits than any other behavior problem. This is sad, because Pugs can be housetrained. Unfortunately, for too many dog owners, housetraining seems to be incredibly difficult. But it doesn't have to be.

Pugs Can Be Housetrained

I am amazed at the number of Pug owners and, unfortunately, even Pug breeders who have Pugs who are not well housetrained. *Housetraining*, the process of teaching a dog where he should and should not relieve himself, is difficult if the Pug's owner makes excuses about it or if she really believes in her heart that

Pug Speak

Housetraining is the process of teaching your dog where he should and should not relieve himself as well as teaching him a verbal command that means he should try to go.

housetraining is impossible. But thousands of well-housetrained Pugs contradict those beliefs. There's absolutely no reason why a Pug shouldn't be reliably house-trained.

I'm not sure how Pugs first got the reputation for being difficult to housetrain. A breed of dogs origi-nally bred to be companions to people would not have survived (or continued as companions) if the dogs could not be reliably housetrained. This breed's rich heritage as companion dogs speaks more eloquently than anything else: Pugs can be housetrained!

Although young puppies can begin to learn housetraining skills, they should never be considered fully housetrained until they're grown up both mentally and physically. That means the housetrain-ing process should continue for

Pug Smarts

If people, even Pug breeders, try to tell you Pugs can't be housetrained, don't listen! They might have failed at housetraining them-selves, but that doesn't mean you have to. Your Pug can be reliably housetrained without a lot of fuss, muss, or difficulty.

at least the first 2 to 3 years of the Pug's life. Not just a few weeks or even months—2 to 3 full years. If the Pug's owner slacks off and doesn't pay attention, the dog can easily begin making mistakes. Those mistakes can then become bad habits, and all the previous housetraining efforts will have been in vain.

The Importance of a Crate

A crate (often called a travel kennel or kennel crate) is a travel car-rier for dogs and other small animals. Originally used for transport-ing animals, crates are now used to help dogs learn housetraining skills. A crate works by taking advantage of the puppy's own instincts to keep his bed clean. Very few puppies or dogs will voluntarily soil their bed, so they learn (with your help) to not go in their bed.

Types of Crates

There are three basic types of crates available, and each has its own good points and bad points. Look at your needs and the needs of your Pug, and decide which one will work best for the both of you.

Watch Out!
Pet store puppies often have trouble with crate training because they spend too much time in a cage. Because they must relieve themselves in the pet store cage, they lose their inhibition about soiling their bed.

The first and most popular type of crate is made of plastic or fiberglass. It has a metal barred door in the front and barred windows for ventilation on each side and often in the back, too. These crates usually come in two pieces (top and bottom) that fasten together about halfway up the sides. These crates are relatively lightweight, although they can be quite bulky. Because these crates have solid sides, they create a "cave" atmosphere and can become the dog's bed and a place of security.

Heavy-gauge wire crates are more like a cage than the plastic crates appear to be, although both confine the dog. The open sides provide good air circulation, and in hot weather, this is very important for Pugs. However, because these cages are more open, some dogs feel more vulnerable and exposed. These crates are also very heavy. Most do fold flat to make storage easier.

Watch Out!
The Pug's extremely short nose can cause breathing difficulties in hot, humid weather. Keeping your Pug cool is very important.

The third type of crate is often called a carry bag rather than a crate. These soft-sided bags are good for carrying toy breed dogs and cats. These can be very useful for transporting a small dog to the veterinarian's office or groomer's salon, but most Pugs are too heavy to be carried easily. With the soft sides, these bags don't work well for housetraining; they are better used for short trips when the dog needs to be carried.

Pug Smarts

You might want to have a wire crate for the summer when your Pug needs more air circulation to keep cool and a plastic crate for the winter when heat is more important.

Crate Size

The crate should be big enough that your Pug can stand up, turn around, lie down, and stretch out. Anything larger than this will allow the puppy to relieve himself in the back of the crate and still be able to get away from it. The purpose of the crate is to teach your dog to hold it and to develop bowel and bladder control by making use of his instinct to keep his bed clean.

Watch Out!

Your Pug shouldn't be crated all night and then again all day. The amount of time he spends in the crate during the day will vary according to his age and the individual dog, but no dog should spend all day crated.

Your Pug's Place

As your Pug gets to know his crate, it will become his own special place. It will be his den or cave, a place where he can hide his toys and retreat to some quiet. He will sleep in the crate at night and nap in it during the day.

Keep It Positive!

Never use the crate for punishment. Never put your Pug in his crate as you are scolding him. Never yell at him or berate him while he's in the crate. Not only will this teach him that the crate is a bad place, but those types of corrections are not good dog training techniques.

Introducing the Crate

How you introduce your Pug to his new crate will determine how he perceives it. If he has a bad first experience with the crate, it will be very difficult to make him rethink that. So it's important you make the crate something fun and the source of good things.

Prop open the door of the crate so it can't slam behind him and startle him. Then have a few dog treats at hand and toss them, one at a time, into the crate. Encourage your Pug to go in after the treats. Do this several times over 2 to 3 days. When your Pug will dash into the crate to get the treats, showing no worry about going in, you can go on to the next step. If your Pug is uneasy, keep tossing treats for another day or two.

 Watch Out!
You have to be sure your Pug's crate training is fun and positive, so plan ahead to prevent any problems.

When your Pug goes in and out of his crate with no trouble, begin feeding him in the crate. Set his food bowl in the back of the crate so he has to step inside to get his food. Keep the door propped open, and let him go in and out as he pleases.

After 2 or 3 meals this way, begin closing the door after your Pug steps inside, then latch the door. If your Pug is calm and quiet after eating, open the door and let him out. If he cries, barks, or throws a temper tantrum, ignore him. Open the door to let him out only when he's calm and quiet and then praise him when he comes out.

Using the Crate

Your Pug should sleep in your bedroom with you but not on your bed. He needs his own place, and that's what the crate will become. Set the crate near your bed where your Pug can be close to you, hear you, and smell you all night long. When he's nearby, you can also hear him if he's restless and needs to go outside.

Most 8- to 12-week-old Pug puppies will need to go outside once during the night. By 12 to 16 weeks of age, most will be able to hold it for 6 to 8 hours while sleeping. Whether your Pug can hold it all night depends on many things. If he ate dinner at 6 and got outside a couple times during the evening, with his last trip outside about 11 P.M., he should be able to hold it until 6 A.M. However, if you go to bed earlier, taking your puppy with you, he will need to get up earlier, too. In addition, if he ate his dinner later, he might need to go outside during the night.

Bet You Didn't Know
Although the crate should never be used to punish your dog, it can be used for "time outs" to interrupt some problem behaviors. When your Pug gets over-stimulated and is not listening to you, quietly, without scolding him, put him in his crate for 15 minutes.

During the day, your Pug can spend some time in the crate for a few minutes here and there. If you need to take a shower, put him in his crate. If you want to wash the kitchen floor, put him in his crate. Put him in his crate whenever you are too busy to supervise him—as long as his time in the crate will only be for 20 to 30 minutes at a time. Your Pug will be spending all night in the crate, so you don't want him to spend all day in it, too.

Don't Abuse It!

As your Pug gets older and develops more bowel and bladder control, he will be able to spend more time in the crate. But be careful about using it too much. He needs time to run and play, chase a ball, and cuddle with you. He should never spend more than 2 to 3 hours in the crate during the day.

A crate is not a jail. It's your dog's special place and a wonderful training tool.

Preventing Problems

The crate can help you with more than housetraining your Pug; it can also help prevent problem behaviors by keeping your Pug from getting into trouble. When you can't supervise him, put him in his crate. You can also put him in an exercise pen or outside in the dog run. Ideally, you should have all three things—crate, exercise pen, and dog run—and rotate where you put your Pug.

Bet You Didn't Know

An exercise pen is portable and can be set up anywhere you need it, outside in the yard or inside your house. It confines your Pug but gives him more room than his crate would.

By preventing bad behavior, your Pug will get into less trouble, cause less damage, and you and your Pug will both be much happier. You can also teach him good behavior by preventing bad behavior. Instead of chewing on your good leather shoes, you can be sure he has one of his toys to munch on.

Housetraining Your Pug

Housetraining your Pug is not difficult, although it does require a great deal of patience on your part as well as some time. You also need to be very consistent with the training, as does everyone else in your household. The process itself, however, is relatively easy. If you understand your Pug's instinct to keep his bed clean, limit his freedom, teach him what you want and where, and set a good schedule, your Pug will cooperate.

Taking Your Pug Outside

When your Pug needs to go outside, take him outside and walk him to the area where you want him to relieve himself. Stand with him, but don't interact with him; this is not a time to play. When he starts to sniff and circle, just watch. After he has started to relieve himself, tell him softly, "Go potty! Good boy to go potty!" (You can use any phrase you want, of course.) When he has finished his business, praise him even more.

Each and every time your Pug needs to go, walk him outside and take him to this spot. Continue to do this for several months—yes, months!

Go outside with your Pug so you can praise him for relieving himself.

During the housetraining process, you cannot send your Pug outside alone. If you do, your training won't work. Your Pug needs to learn the "Go potty!" phrase you're teaching him, and you need to be outside with him to do that. Also, you need to praise him when he does relieve himself, and if you're not outside, you can't praise him immediately. Plus, your Pug wants to be with you; if you send him outside alone, he will stay by the door, hoping you'll come out, too, and he won't relieve himself.

Bet You Didn't Know

Many puppies, including Pugs, want to be with their people so much, they won't take the time to relieve themselves. These puppies will just hold it until they can't hold it anymore and then it's too late to make it to the backyard. When you go outside with your Pug, your Pug doesn't have this problem.

Many Pug owners complain, "I send my dog outside, but when he comes in the house, he runs to the carpet and urinates. Why does he do that when he was just outside?" If this happens, your training has broken down. When your dog is outside alone, you have no idea of whether he's relieved himself or not. So when you let him in, you might be letting him back in with a full bladder. After going two or three times on the carpet, your Pug will think that's where he's supposed to go. After all, you aren't teaching him anything different.

If you go outside with your Pug and he doesn't relieve himself, he shouldn't be allowed back in the house to run around. He either stays outside, or he comes in and goes into his crate. Offer him the chance to go potty again in about 20 minutes. Praise him when he does go.

Housetraining is a very important skill. Take your time teaching this, do what you need to do, and be patient. It will all come together and be well worth your efforts.

Using the "Go Potty" Command

When you go outside with your Pug and tell him, "Go potty" as he relieves himself, you are teaching him a command for that action. He will begin to associate that phrase with the act of relieving himself. This is a very important skill and one you should begin using right away.

Tell your Pug to relieve himself when you're out on walks so he learns both to try to do it on command and do it in different places. Some Pugs learn to go potty in their backyard and then feel they should never go anywhere else. These poor dogs won't go on walks or while traveling but will try to hold it until they just about explode. Teach your Pug that when you give him the "Go potty" command, he is to try, even if he can only squeeze out a few drops!

If you take your Pug with you to visit some friends or relatives, it's very nice to be able to tell your dog to relieve himself prior to going inside their home. You can do the same thing while traveling.

When you stop for gas or for a potty break for yourself, take your Pug for a walk and tell him to relieve himself—and praise him when he does, of course.

Tips for Continuing Housetraining Success

Teaching your Pug to relieve himself outside on command is the beginning of the housetraining process. However, you also need to establish a schedule for going outside. Not only will this help prevent accidents, but it will also help your Pug develop bowel and bladder control as he learns to hold it for gradually increased periods of time. Your Pug also needs to learn how to let you know he needs to go outside, and you must learn to watch his body language so you can get him outside in time.

Pugs Are Creatures of Habit

Pugs, more so than many other breeds of dogs, are creatures of habit and thrive on a regular routine. Nowhere is that routine more important than in housetraining. Housetraining is much easier if the Pug, especially a Pug puppy, eats, sleeps, and goes outside on a regular schedule.

When all activities are on a schedule, you can then plan for the trips outside. Your Pug will need to go outside at set times and after certain activities.

Take your Pug outside when …

- He wakes up after sleeping or napping. Carry him outside if you need to so he doesn't stop along the way.

- He finishes eating.

- He has played for a few minutes. Activity gets everything moving!

- You let him out of his crate after he's been in it for any period of time.

Pug Smarts _____
It your young Pug hasn't had an accident in a while, don't consider him house-trained. Instead, simply pat yourself on the back. You're doing everything right!

Puppies between 8 and 12 weeks old should get outside every hour they're awake during the day and evening. Between 12 and 16 weeks of age, puppies should go out every 2 hours. After that, times and schedules depend on the individual puppy.

When Your Pug's Gotta Go!

Many dog owners assume that a dog should bark at the door when he needs to go outside, but that isn't so. In fact, teaching a dog to bark oftentimes leads to a barking problem later, complete with neighbor complaints. Instead, all your Pug needs to do is communicate with you somehow that he needs to go outside. He can come find you in the house, stare at you, paw at your foot, or dance a jig at your feet. As long as you both understand what he's saying, it doesn't matter how he communicates with you.

You can teach your dog to get excited about going outside by using your voice to encourage him. Say, "Sweetie, do you need to go potty?" as you walk toward the door. If you use a higher-pitched, happy tone of voice, your Pug will look at you, dance a little, and run toward the door. Praise him for going to the door, then once outside, praise him again. Be quiet while he relieves himself (so you don't distract him), then praise him after he's finished. Remember, going outside and going potty are two very good things! Let your voice show it.

As you progress through housetraining, pay attention to your Pug's body language when he needs to go outside. What does he do? When you see what body language he's using to communicate with you that he needs to go, ask him, "Sweetie, do you have to go outside to go potty?" If he has to go, he will head to the door. If he doesn't, he might just look at you.

As your Pug gets older, he will learn to come to you when he needs to go out. Always praise him when he does. Don't expect this right away, though. It takes maturity for the dog to learn to ask you for help. Some Pugs don't reach this point for a year or more. Just continue to talk to your dog as you take him outside. It will all come together one day.

No Excuses!

I think one reason so many Pugs are not well housetrained is because many Pug owners can be wonderful about making excuses. It's so easy to say, "But Pugs just don't housetrain well!" or "Pugs are very slow to mature and don't pick up on housetraining until they're *(fill in the age)*." But excuses are just that: excuses. Pugs *do* housetrain well. There is absolutely no reason to have a nonhousetrained Pug.

This doesn't mean that accidents won't happen; they will. But most of the time, those accidents will be *your* fault. If your puppy is in the room with you, you might get distracted and forget to take him outside in time and he will urinate on the floor. Or perhaps you will be in the shower and forget to put the puppy in the crate.

When an accident does happen, how you handle it is very important. Don't scold the puppy for the puddle on the floor or the pile on the carpet. After all, he has to go; that's not wrong. What was wrong was where he went. So no rubbing his nose in the mess, and no scolding him after the fact. Simply put him outside in a safe, protected place (such as in a covered dog run or a covered patio) and go back inside and clean it up. Then promise him you'll pay more attention next time.

Bet You Didn't Know
Clean up any accidents with white vinegar, and use it liberally. It will get rid of any odors that might bring your dog back to that spot again.

If you come upon the puppy as he is going, you can verbally scold him, "Oh no!" and then grab him and take him outside. Interrupting him as he's doing it is fine (you can chastise him then), but scolding him after the fact is worthless. He won't understand what he's being punished for.

If your Pug puppy is having several accidents a week, you're doing something wrong. My youngest dog, Riker, had only one accident in the house from the time I brought him home at 8 weeks of age. Just one accident. If your puppy is making a lot of mistakes, you need to take a serious look at how you're doing housetraining him:

🏠 How often are you taking your Pug outside?

🏠 Is he going out after naps, after eating, and after playtimes?

🏠 Are you going out with him and praising him?

🏠 Are you limiting his freedom in the house?

🏠 When have the accidents happened?

Watch Out!

If you Pug has been well housetrained and suddenly begins having accidents, take him to the veterinarian's office to be sure a health problem isn't causing the accidents.

Take a look at all the information you have and try to figure out where the training process failed, then work from there to fix it.

Pug Speak

A **doggy door** is a small door (or flap) installed in a door that allow your Pug to go in and out as he pleases without any help from you.

Doggy Doors

Doggy doors can be effective for adult dogs who are left alone for many hours each day. The dog can go outside to relieve himself and then come back in the house when he's done.

Doggy doors are not a good idea for puppies because the door will eliminate you from the training process and give the pup too much freedom. The puppy will go outside without you, and you won't be able to teach him the "Go potty" command, nor will you be able to praise him for relieving himself. In addition, when he comes in, you won't have any idea whether he's relieved himself or not.

However, when your Pug has been well housetrained for a period of time and responds to your verbal command to relieve himself, you can introduce a doggy door for convenience, especially if you are gone for several hours during the day. However, even then, do not let your Pug have free run through the door all the time. Close it at night (this will also keep nocturnal critters from coming into the house), and close it during the day while you're home with your dog. You still want the dog to keep his house-training skills sharp, including coming to get you when he needs to go outside.

Watch Out!

If you live in an area populated with birds of prey or other predators, be sure the doggy door opens to a secure, covered dog run.

Dog Litter Boxes

Litter boxes for dogs have been in use for many years, especially for toy breed dogs. Most dog owners who use them just use cat litter boxes and cat litter, which can work very well. However, in the last few years, commercial dog litter boxes and dog litter have become available. The boxes are usually a little bigger, with slightly deeper sides than cat boxes, and the litter itself is different.

I'm not a fan of dog litter boxes except in a few specific situations. In some cases, teaching the Pug to use a box in the house seems to teach him that relieving himself in the house is okay (anywhere in the house) rather than specifically in the box in the house.

However, litter boxes can work if …

🏠 The owner is housebound or unable to walk their Pug.

🏠 The dog and owner live in a climate where the weather would be dangerous for a Pug.

🏠 The owner works long hours and the dog must remain in the house all day with no one to take him outside.

If the dog and owner are able to go outside on a regular basis, I much prefer teaching the Pug to relieve himself outside. It's easier, usually more reliable, and more natural to the dog.

If you decide that a dog litter box would work better for you than taking your dog outside, follow all the housetraining directions except instead of taking your dog outside, you'll take him to his box. All the other directions still apply.

Be Patient

All puppies need time to grow and develop bladder and bowel control, so be patient with your puppy's housetraining. Set up a schedule that works for both you and your Pug, then stick with it. Just remember, a lack of accidents doesn't mean you can slack off. It just means you're doing everything right. Keep it up!

The Least You Need to Know

🏠 Pugs can be housetrained, so don't listen to people who tell you otherwise.

🏠 A crate is a wonderful housetraining tool that helps teach your Pug bowel and bladder control.

🏠 Pugs are creatures of habit, so establish a schedule for eating, sleeping, playtimes, and outside potty times.

🏠 Be patient. Housetraining takes time.

Chapter 7

The Social Pug

In This Chapter

- 🏠 Socializing your Pug
- 🏠 How and when to socialize
- 🏠 Watching for fear periods
- 🏠 Continuing socialization into adulthood

I have mentioned throughout this book that Pugs were bred to be companions for people. Hearing this, many new Pug owners believe that Pugs are born well adapted to life with people. Unfortunately, this isn't true. Pugs are born knowing Pugs; puppies imprint on their mother and on the breeder, if the breeder is active with the puppies. Granted, Pugs are born with the ability to live with people, but this doesn't happen automatically.

All dogs, even Pugs, need socialization. A well-socialized Pug will bond well with his owners and will look upon visitors, friends, and family as interesting creatures, not something to fear or defend their people against. A well-socialized Pug thinks life with people is quite amusing!

What Is Socialization?

Socialization is a planned process of introducing a puppy to the world around him. This shouldn't be undertaken in a haphazard manner; it is much too important to happen when time permits or when an occasion arises that's convenient for you. Socialization must be planned, and you must make time in your busy schedule.

An important part of the process is introducing the puppy to people. When a puppy meets people of all sizes, shapes, ages, and ethnicities, he will be less apt to shy away from people who are different. For example, many dogs who are raised in a household with only adults are very worried about children. They can be shy, fearful, or even aggressive when children approach them. It's important that puppies meet people in all their infinite varieties.

> **Pug Speak**
> **Socialization** is the process of introducing a dog to the world around him, beginning as a puppy and continuing into adulthood.

Socialization encompasses more than people, though. It also includes introducing puppies to other animals and to the sights, sounds, and smells of the world.

The Importance of Socialization

A well-socialized Pug will be bold, confident, and able to cope with the world around him. A Pug who has not been exposed to the sights, sounds, and smells of the world, as well as a variety of people and other animals, will not have the same confidence and skills and could potentially develop behavior problems.

Recently I had two Pugs enroll in one of my basic obedience classes. These two puppies were littermates, just over 4 months old, and both fawn females. When I called the breeder, who lives locally and is well known in the Pug world, she said when the puppies left her house for their new homes both were 10 weeks old, confident, and self-assured.

Bet You Didn't Know

The more the puppy sees, smells, and hears as a puppy (without being frightened), the better he will cope when faced with challenges as an adult.

I will call the first puppy Sally (her name changed to protect the owner's identity). Before beginning the obedience class, Sally had been on walks around her neighborhood and had met the neighbor's children and a few well-behaved, well-vaccinated neighborhood dogs. Sally had even met a neighbor's cat and rabbit. After she had two sets of vaccinations, Sally's owner had taken her to the local park and a pet supply store, where a clerk gave Sally a doggy treat. Sally walked into class on leash, was eager to greet me, and was friendly with the other dogs and people in class.

The second Pug puppy I'll call Molly (again, name changed to protect the owner's identity). Other than two trips to the vet's office, Molly had stayed home after leaving the breeder's home. She had not met any other dogs, nor had she seen any other animals, and she had not been introduced to any children. Molly had made two car trips to the veterinarian's office, and the second time was very fearful. The veterinarian had told Molly's owner to call me for training, saying Molly was on course to develop behavior problems.

Molly's owner had kept her home because she felt she was protecting her puppy. She knew Molly was very small and kept her away from larger dogs and children so she wouldn't get hurt. She kept Molly away from other dogs, too, so she wouldn't get sick. By being so protective, however, Molly's owner also deprived Molly of a chance to build her confidence and learn coping skills. Molly should have been as bold and self-assured as her sister, but she wasn't.

Sally had a great time in class. She learned quickly and visited with other dogs and people in class. Molly was so afraid that she couldn't learn. Her owner, seeing her fear, kept picking her up so she could protect her. Even though Molly needed the socialization a group class can provide, I referred Molly's owner to private dog training lessons first so she could learn what she was doing to her dog. I hoped that she could relax then and allow Molly to socialize with friendly dogs and people.

Even Social Pugs Need Socialization

Pug puppies are fearless and self-assured, as Molly and Sally's breeder said, but without socialization, that attitude will change. As we saw with Molly, even confident Pugs will wilt and become fearful if they're not exposed to people, animals, and the sights, sounds, and smells of the world.

Some Pug owners enjoy socializing with other Pug owners, allowing their Pugs to have playtimes together. This is great socialization, but Pug owners should remember their Pugs need to meet dogs of other breeds, too. Just as Pugs should meet people in all their variety, they should also meet dogs of all sizes, shapes, colors, and conformation. Just be sure the dogs are healthy, friendly, and well-vaccinated.

Watch Out!

You must take time to do the socialization needed when your Pug is a puppy. You cannot make up for this later.

Socialization in the Wild vs. at Home

In wild canines—wolves, coyotes, or even feral dogs—a pup is raised in his family pack and learns to identify those individuals. He doesn't have to get along with anyone else, and in fact, learns that strangers mean danger. In our world, however, a dog must be able to tolerate other people, including neighbors, friends, the meter reader, the postal carrier, and the newspaper delivery person.

And when that wild canine grows up and begins to hunt, he will only hunt within his home range. Rarely will he cross into another wild canine's range. However, when we walk our dogs, they are constantly walking across or past other dogs' scent markings, thereby crossing into another dog's territory. We also take our dogs camping, hiking, and traveling—all of which occur outside your Pug's home territory. People don't follow dogs' rules at all! Some insecure male dogs will react by marking (leg-lifting and urinating) on every upright object. Other dogs will be very fearful and submissive, especially in the presence of other dogs. Early socialization can prevent much of this confusion.

How and When to Socialize

Begin socialization a few days after you bring home your Pug puppy. Give him a few days to get to know you and your immediate family and for you to begin his housetraining. After about 3 or 4 days, let him begin to meet new people. Take him outside, and, one at a time, let him meet your neighbors, your neighbor's young children (including babies and toddlers), the teenagers skateboarding past, and the retirees strolling down your street.

When people meet your Pug puppy, keep control of the situation. You want your Pug to think new people are exciting, friendly, fun, and nonthreatening. Don't let anyone manhandle your Pug or play roughly with him. If someone gets too rough, just take your Pug away.

 Watch Out!

Be sure your Pug meets people of all ages, sizes, and ethnic backgrounds. You don't want him to shy away from people who are different.

Your puppy can also meet other animals as long as they are friendly toward puppies. Let him meet a friendly cat, have him sniff a pet rabbit, and let him peek at a neighbor's bearded dragon (a lizard) in its cage. Just be sure to control your Pug so he doesn't get hurt or cause himself or the other critter any harm.

Your Pug needs to meet many nice, friendly, gentle people.

Once your puppy has had at least two sets of vaccinations (talk to your veterinarian about a shot schedule), let him begin meeting other friendly, well-vaccinated dogs. Don't be shy about asking other people whether their dogs are up to date on vaccinations; it's your responsibility to protect your Pug. (I'll talk more about this in Chapter 11.)

Watch Out!

Don't assume an adult dog is well vaccinated. To protect your puppy, be proactive and ask the dog's owner.

Sights, Smells, Sounds, and Textures

Socialization is more than just meeting other people, animals, and dogs; it's also about seeing, smelling, hearing, and touching different things. Puppies should use their senses to discover the world; they should see, smell, hear, and touch new things and discover what those things are. Socialization is also all about discovering the world.

In the house, be sure your puppy hears a variety of everyday sounds. Not all at once, of course!

- A vacuum cleaner
- A dishwasher
- A garbage disposal and trash compactor
- A plastic garbage bag being shook open
- A plastic bag being popped
- A paper bag being crumbled
- A broom and mop being used
- A metal pan lid dropped on the floor

Outside, your puppy should hear the following:

- A car engine being revved
- A trash truck picking up trash
- A motorcycle driving down the street
- A lawn mower
- A weed whacker and a leaf blower

In addition to new sights, smells, and sounds, introduce your Pug to different textures and surfaces:

- Carpet
- Slippery floors
- Floor mats and carpet runners
- Stairs
- Metal manhole covers
- Dirt, sand, and gravel
- Concrete and asphalt

Let your Pug see, hear, smell, and touch different things, places, and people.

Don't forget the everyday things you might not think about immediately. How about kids' toys? Some toys make some really strange sounds that could easily startle a dog who is not used to them. Be sure your Pug puppy sees, hears, and gets to investigate a variety of different things.

Keep It Happy!

Good socialization should build confidence and make your Pug bold and confidant. To do this, keep all your Pug's socialization experiences happy. When you're introducing something new, use a happy tone of voice, saying, "Sweetie, come see the rabbit!"

Keep a handful of doggy treats in your pocket, and should something appear to startle your Pug, bring out a treat, not to reward the startle but to counteract it. If the UPS delivery person scares your

Pug, hand the treat to the delivery person and ask him to give it to your Pug. He'll be more than happy to have a canine customer who doesn't want to bite him!

When something startles your puppy, say in a happy tone of voice, "What was that?" and when you can, walk him up to it. Touch the motorcycle or flapping sheet on the clothesline, and encourage your puppy to come close to see that it really isn't scary. When he's brave, praise him!

Bet You Didn't Know

Your Pug's adult personality is shaped by several things: his breed and genetic heritage, his mother's care, the socialization and training he receives, and you.

What *Not* to Do

Overwhelming your Pug by trying to introduce him to everything all at once is just as bad as not socializing him at all. As I mentioned in the beginning of this chapter, plan your Pug's socialization. In his first few days at home, let him get used to the family and the sights, sounds, and smells of his new home. By the end of the first week, take him outside to meet a few of the neighbors and to get to know the neighborhood.

Each week, take your puppy to a few more places:

Bet You Didn't Know

Do not hug and coddle your Pug if he's frightened by something. You might think you're reassuring him, but your Pug is going to think you're praising him for his fear.

- 🏠 Go for a walk past the local elementary school, and ask one or two of the kids (not a crowd!) to pet your Pug.

- 🏠 Walk along the local beach, and let him smell the ocean and watch the seagulls.

❧ Stroll past a nursing home or retirement center, and let some of the residents pet him. (This will do both of them some good!)

❧ Go to the pet supply store.

In any scenarios you take your Pug, you must control the situation. Don't let kids run and scream, and don't let too many people gang up on your puppy. Be sure no one grabs your puppy and hugs him too hard. And of course, never let anyone treat him roughly.

Fear Periods

Puppies go through several *fear periods* during their development. Puppies demonstrate their fear in different ways. Some will be very cautious, approaching things, even known objects, tentatively. Other puppies will be more selective, acting bold about some things and cautious about others.

A friend's Pug puppy demonstrated that he was in a fear period when he walked out their back door to go potty one morning and began barking at their kids' swing set. The swing set had been there since before he joined the family, but it was as if he had never seen it before and found it very menacing. My friend had to walk her Pug puppy up to the swing set and touch it before he would stop barking at it.

Pug Speak

A **fear period** is a period of time when your puppy is more apt to view things around him as frightening.

If a puppy is severely frightened of something during a fear period, that fear potentially could remain with the puppy for his lifetime.

Common Fear Period Ages

The first fear period occurs when the puppy's 8 weeks old, usually when he leaves his original home and travels by car to his new home. Most puppies also go to the veterinarian's office this week, too. All those new things can be very scary, and this is, for most puppies, the strongest fear period. Almost all puppies react in one way or another, being afraid of car rides or the veterinarian's office for many years.

To avoid a trauma such as this, many Pug breeders prefer to keep their puppies until they are 10 weeks old. Even if you brought home your puppy at 7 or 8 weeks of age, don't worry. He will still be able to bond with you and your family.

The second fear period usually hits when the puppy is 4 to 5 months old. Many behaviorists believe that between 60 and 75 percent of all puppies have some type of a fearful reaction at this age.

The third period often occurs when puppies are about 14 months old. Fewer puppies suffer from this one than the two previous, with probably 30 to 50 percent of all puppies having problems at this age. Although 14-month-old dogs aren't normally considered puppies, they should be because they are still mentally immature.

Coping With Fear Periods

Fear periods can be just as scary for puppy owners as they are for puppies. When a formerly confident puppy is suddenly frightened of normal, everyday things, even an experienced dog owner can be flustered. But you can do several things to make this easier; after all, it is a normal part of the puppy's development.

First of all, don't reinforce your Pug puppy's fears. If you save him by cuddling and coddling him, he will feel that his fears were justified. So don't hold him close and tell him, "It's okay, sweetie.

Don't worry," in a soft, soothing voice. Instead, use a calm, matter-of-fact voice or a happy, fun tone of voice and say, "Hey! What are you barking at? You're so silly!"

Watch Out!

Don't praise or reinforce fear, even inadvertently. This will cause your dog to become more fearful and could continue for his lifetime.

You can distract your puppy by turning him away from what scared him, using your voice, and offering him a toy or a treat when he's looking elsewhere, such as, "Where's your ball?" Puppies have a short attention span, and distracting them is usually quite easy.

If the object of his fear is accessible, walk him up to it, touch it, and show him it isn't as scary as he thought. Walk up to the swing set, touch it, move a swing slightly (not a lot), and tell your puppy, "Hey! Look!" in a fun tone of voice. If he walks up to it, praise him, saying "Good boy to be brave!"

Pug Smarts

When you're out and about, use dog treats liberally to reinforce brave behavior.

Don't drag him up to the object of his fear, though. If he's hesitant, let him sit back and watch you be brave. When you touch it and nothing happens, he might decide to follow you. When he does, praise him.

The fear period at 8 weeks is the hardest, the one at 4 months isn't quite as bad, and the one at 14 months is the easiest. But if your Pug puppy happens to hit all three, don't worry. Jolly your Pug through them, and know that they are temporary.

Don't stop your socialization efforts when your puppy is going through a fear period. Instead, continue taking him out and about. Just be ready to deal with his fear, should it appear.

Planning Socialization

As much as possible, plan out your Pug's socialization. If it's easier for you, make a list:

- ❏ Has your Pug heard and seen the trash truck?

- ❏ Has he watched and heard your neighbor's motorcycle go down the street?

- ❏ Have you taken him to the local elementary school as the kids leave to go home in the afternoon?

By making a plan and a checklist, you can be sure you've done everything possible to expose your Pug to the world he's living in.

My grandmother always said that parents should raise their children to take the path they want them to follow as adults. It's the same with puppies. Raise your puppy to walk that path with you. If you like to go places and do things, introduce your Pug to those things now, and when he's grown up, he'll be right there by your side.

Socialization should last into adulthood.

Continuing Socialization

Although socialization is most important during puppyhood, beginning from 10 weeks of age on, the process should not stop as your puppy grows up. Dogs, especially Pugs, should never be isolated; it is not a natural state for them.

My husband and I have dogs because we enjoy them. We cherish their company and love to plan activities for both ourselves and our dogs. On any given weekend, we might take the dogs to do agility, go to a park for a picnic, or play at the beach. Our dogs have splashed in the ocean, sniffed noses with a Budweiser Clydesdale, visited with Alzheimer's patients, and ridden on a San Francisco cable car. They have hiked in the Sierra Nevada Mountains, walked through the forests of the Appalachian Mountains, hiked in meadows, and explored deserts. They have attended county fairs and walked in local Christmas parades. And they take it all in stride.

When Your Veterinarian Disagrees

Your veterinarian might tell your to keep your Pug puppy home until he's had all his vaccinations. Until then, he might be at risk of picking up a contagious disease from unvaccinated, unhealthy dogs. In this chapter, however, I have emphasized the importance of early socialization. Obviously, there is a disagreement here.

Your veterinarian is concerned about your puppy's health, and he or she has a justifiable concern. As a dog trainer, I'm concerned about the serious consequences of a lack of socialization.

Unsocialized dogs run the risk of developing severe behavior problems, including uncontrollable fears and fear-based aggression. Granted, not all unsocialized Pugs become fear-biters, nor are all fear-biters unsocialized. However, there is a strong enough relationship to show that socialization must be begun in puppyhood. The other advantages of socialization are just frosting on the cake.

You can socialize your puppy and cut down on the risks of exposing him to diseases. First, when he's still getting his first two sets of vaccinations, don't take him to places where there are a lot of dogs. (I'll discuss vaccinations in greater detail in Chapter 11.) Don't go to dog parks or dog walks. Don't let him sniff where other dogs have relieved themselves, as many canine diseases can be passed through urine and feces. And don't let him play with other dogs until you have asked their owners about their dogs' vaccinations. Be sure the dogs are healthy and up to date on their shots.

Watch Out!

It's up to you to protect your puppy, so be forward when you need to be. Ask other dog owners questions before your dogs sniff each other. "When were your dog's last shots?" If the dog owners get upset, too bad! It's your puppy's health, and you have every right to protect him.

Don't enroll your Pug puppy in a kindergarten puppy class until he's had at least two full sets of vaccinations. Most dog trainers require this before starting class anyway, but be sure the trainer observes this policy.

You can decrease the chances of your Pug puppy getting sick by being aware and careful, yet still provide the socialization he needs for good mental health.

The Least You Need to Know

- 🐾 Make a plan to socialize your Pug; it's vitally important to your Pug's good mental health.

- 🐾 Begin socialization early, and introduce your Pug to a variety of sights, sounds, and smells.

- 🐾 Fear periods are normal. Don't give in to them.

- 🐾 Socialization should continue through puppyhood and into adulthood.

Chapter 8

Have Fun with Your Pug!

In This Chapter

- 🏠 Playing with your Pug
- 🏠 Games your Pug will love
- 🏠 Exercising your Pug (and you!)
- 🏠 Walking with your Pug

Recently I watched my 5-year-old nephew, Adam, as he played with his small toy cars and trucks. He created traffic patterns as he made the cars zoom past each other, complete with amazing sound effects. He took a toy Porsche off-roading through the grass and then staged a really horrific accident with cars piled on top of each other. He was having a great time all by himself, but when my brother-in-law sat down to play with him, the game became even more fun. Shared play is more than twice as exciting.

A puppy, especially a funny Pug puppy, is an excellent reason to rediscover the joys of playing. Playing with your puppy is a wonderful way to bond with your puppy, and it's a great way for the both of you to get some exercise, too.

Make Time to Play

Children and puppies naturally want to play, but when people grow up, they tend to lose some of that desire to play. We get serious about life and focus on work more than fun, and what fun we do have tends to have the potential to be destructive—fast motor vehicles or potentially dangerous sports like rock climbing. But simple play that makes us laugh is very good for us, both mentally and physically.

In puppies, play is preparation for adulthood. When your puppy plays with you, you can teach him how to play and that he shouldn't use his teeth on your skin when you're playing (or ever!). You can teach him games, such as how to bring back toys that you throw. When you play with your puppy, you are having fun with him but you're also teaching him and providing leadership.

The hardest part of this for some puppy owners is actually taking (or making) the time to play. It's so easy to tell the puppy, "Not now, sweetie, I need to take out the trash." Or, "Not now. I have to cook dinner." Face it: There is always something that needs to be done. But your Pug will be a puppy a very short period of time, and if he keeps asking you to play by bringing you his toys or by *play bowing* at your feet and you continue to say no, unfortunately, he will eventually stop asking you to play.

Pug Speak

Puppies and even adult dogs invite another dog or a person to play by **play bowing**. The dog lowers his front end, with his front legs outstretched, while his hips remain high and his tail wagging wildly.

A puppy who needs to play and has no one to play with will invent his own games—and you might not like the games he comes up with! My first dog as an adult was a German Shepherd named Watachie. I was single, living alone, and worked 8 hours a day, so Watachie was home alone for many hours. When he was about

4½ months old, I came home one evening to find my sofa in shreds. Watachie had spent the day tearing the fabric and stuffing off the sofa. He had a great time! I wasn't there to play with him, so he invented his own game. I left him alone too long, I had made another mistake, too: I allowed him too much freedom. I learned two lessons from that episode.

You don't have to dedicate huge amounts of time to playing with your Pug. What's more important is that you take the time when you can. A few minutes here and there is fine. For example, my dogs know that while I'm working at the computer, they are not to disturb me unless they have to go outside. But when I get up from the computer, I'm fair game and the dogs know it. They'll bring me toys to share or a ball to throw. When I walk out in the garden, I'll throw a Frisbee or play hide-and-seek. I might also do some trick training, because that's fun for both my dogs and me. A few minutes here and there, complete with some laughter and exercise, is great—for both of you!

Good for You and Your Pug

The past two decades have produced quite a lot of research on the effects of exercise, play, and laughter on our health. We know exercise is good for us; that's been reiterated time after time. We also know we probably don't always get enough exercise.

But researchers have also found that play itself is good. Play, in the form of either physical or mental games, has a beneficial effect on both our mind and body. Physical play, like exercise, keeps the blood moving and the muscles working, and releases endorphins in the bloodstream. We feel good after playing. Both physical play and mental play (such as board

Bet You Didn't Know

Norman Cousins was the instigator into research about the positive effects of laughter. During a hospital stay, he began watching funny movies and found that he felt better after he'd been laughing.

games or games like charades) keep our minds active because we have to think about what we're doing. And of course that's good for us.

When you play with your Pug, not only do these beneficial things happen to you, but they also happen to your dog. Your Pug gets some exercise during physical play, and even if it isn't strenuous, your dog is still moving and stretching his muscles. When you laugh, your Pug will react to you and will play bow, wagging his tail and asking for more play.

Pug Speak

When a dog and owner are **bonded** to each other, they care about each other. The dog is definitely one of the family.

When you first bring home your Pug, either a puppy or an adult, playing gently with him will help build a *bond* between the two of you. Dogs and people don't automatically bond with each other; the bond comes with caring about each other and time spent together. Later, playing together will help keep that bond firm.

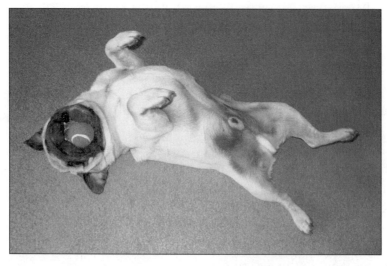

Make time to play with your Pug. It's good for both of you.

Games to Play

You can play many games with your Pug. Some are games dog owners have played with their dogs for as long as we've had a relationship between the species, such as retrieving a thrown object. You can also make up some games you and your Pug discover together.

Here are some games I've enjoyed with my dogs:

- **Tug-of-war.** Tug-of-war games have gotten a bad reputation from dog trainers and behaviorists because many believe this game can cause aggressive behavior as well as escalate dominance issues. They are probably correct; in some dogs, either of those issues could be true. However, you can play tug-of-war with your Pug safely, without causing any issues, as long as *you* always win the game, not your Pug. You must be able to tell your Pug, "That's enough," and be able to take away the toy. When you want your Pug to let go of the toy, ask him to sit and then offer him a treat. When he lets go of the toy for the treat, praise him, saying, "Good boy to let go!" Always play this game gently. Remember, Pugs are sturdy but not big. You don't want to hurt his jaws or teeth.

- **Retrieving games.** Dogs have been chasing thrown sticks forever. Pugs are not always good at retrieving games, unfortunately, but it's worth teaching them because when your dog does enjoy it, it's great fun. In addition, chasing after a toy is good exercise for your Pug. Begin introducing your Pug to an item you'll throw by playing tug-of-war with it (soft rope toys are good for this). Make it exciting, praise your dog for grabbing it, then pull it back and forth. Ask your dog to drop it, and when he does, toss the toy just a few feet away. When he goes after it, praise him and then encourage him to bring it back to you. You can gradually throw the toy farther away.

- **Hide-and-seek.** Have a family member hold the dog as you run and hide. Then, from your hiding spot, call your dog while your family member releases him and says, "Go find sister!"

When you're found, you should both praise your dog. In the beginning, the person holding the dog might need to help the dog search. Eventually, the dog will learn the game and will learn to check all the hiding spots all by himself. This game also teaches the dog the names of family members.

The name game. Take two of the Pug's toys (such as a ball and a bone) and a handful of special doggy treats, then sit on the floor. Hold the ball in front of the Pug, and encourage him to sniff it or touch it as you say, "Ball!" Then give him a treat. Do this several times until he willingly touches the ball as you say its name and then turns for the treat. Next, repeat the exercise with the bone. Then place both toys on the floor in front of you and say, "Ball!" If he moves toward the ball, praise him and pop a treat in his mouth. Do the same thing with the bone. When he knows these two toys, begin adding new toys and their names over several training sessions.

Shake hands and wave. Trick training is great fun, both for you and for your dog. Pugs love to show off for a crowd, and trick training is a wonderful way to do that. The first trick most people teach their dog is usually to shake. Sit your Pug in front of you, and as you tell him, "Sweetie, shake," tickle the back of his paw. As he lifts his paw away from that tickle, touch it with your hand and praise him. Pop a treat in his mouth. When he's reliably lifting his paw as you ask him to shake, stop tickling. When he knows the shake well, you can convert it to a wave by not touching his raised paw. You can convert this command by saying, "Shake, wave," first and eventually saying only, "Sweetie, wave."

It really doesn't matter what games you play with your dog or what tricks you teach him. What is important is that the two of you spend time together doing something fun and having a good time doing it.

Exercise Is Necessary for Good Health

Although playing games with your Pug can be good exercise, especially retrieving and tug-of-war games, play alone is not always enough exercise for good health.

The importance of exercise cannot be dismissed. Just as exercise keeps us healthy (or healthier), it can do the same for your Pug. Exercise keeps his body strong and improves his immune system. It keeps his muscles taut and his body's systems working as they should. Although many Pug owners are quick to say their Pug is a couch potato—and many Pugs would prefer to remain that way—some exercise should be a part of the daily routine:

- A Pug puppy can get enough exercise by playing vigorously in the house and yard and then going for a walk. The speed and distance of the walk should be tailored to the puppy's age and ability to walk on a leash.

- A young, healthy, adult Pug will need some good aerobic exercise in addition to the play times and walks.

- A mature Pug will do well with some play, a good walk, and a little additional aerobic exercise.

- A senior Pug should have some playtime and a good walk, with the walking distance and speed tailored to his abilities.

What Kind of Exercise?

With their short legs and even shorter noses, Pugs are not and never will be star canine athletes. They shouldn't be jogging partners or run with bicycles as so many other longer-legged dogs do so easily. However, a strong and healthy Pug can easily walk several miles each day.

Exercise is necessary for good physical and mental health.

Pugs can also participate in some dog sports and activities, including the following:

🏠 **Agility.** Although the shining stars of this sport are usually Border Collies, Shetland Sheepdogs, and Australian Shepherds, Pugs can have a great time in agility. The sport consists of a variety of jumps and obstacles that the dog must run through, climb, or jump over. The heights of the jumps vary according to the height of the dog, so Pugs don't have to jump as high as the larger breeds do. Many trainers have agility courses, so check with a trainer near you.

🏠 **Carting.** Many craft and toy stores sell very small red wagons that have a bed only about 14 inches long. These lightweight wagons are great for toy breed dogs. You can remove the handle and replace it with a set of wagon shafts, and you can pad a cat harness with some fleece to make a small pulling harness for your Pug. Don't put any weight in the wagon, though. The training itself and pulling the little wagon will give your Pug enough exercise.

Flyball. Flyball is a team relay race. Each team has four dogs who, one at a time, jump a series of four hurdles, then pounce on a board that tosses out a tennis ball. The dog then turns and races back over the hurdles to the starting point, and the next dog then runs the course. Most teams like to have at a least one small dog because the hurdle heights are then lowered to accommodate the small dog. Some Pugs' mouths are too small for a normal-size tennis ball, but if your Pug can grab it, this is a fun sport.

Exercise can also be as simple as running around the backyard with your Pug or as elaborate as going for a half-day hike in a local wilderness area. Chose activities that are interesting, because if you get bored, you'll quit. You don't have to do the same thing every day, either. Have fun with what you and your Pug are doing, and you're more apt to continue doing it.

How Much Exercise Is Enough?

Just as every person's fitness level is different, so is every Pug's, and you really need to know your Pug to determine how much exercise is enough. If your Pug's breathing hard after an exercise session, that's okay. If his breathing is labored and his sides are heaving, that's too much. You should expect your Pug to be somewhat tired after exercise, but if he's too tired to walk, he's done too much.

You'll be able to monitor your Pug's activities by his fitness. Pugs are stocky dogs with a blocky body; they will never be as sleek and thin as a Greyhound. However, even Pugs should not be fat. If your Pug is stocky, with hard muscles and just a little meat over his ribs, and he can play vigorously without getting too out of breath, he's fit.

Watch Out!
Pugs have difficulty breathing when the weather is hot and humid. In this weather, cut back on the outdoor activities and keep play sessions inside in the air conditioning.

Begin all exercise programs slowly, however, because sore muscles are no fun. If your Pug hasn't exercised for a while, you might want to get him checked out with your veterinarian before beginning an exercise regime.

If you have owned a more athletic breed of dogs prior to getting a Pug, be cautious with your play and exercise sessions until you get to know your Pug. Labrador Retrievers, Golden Retrievers, and the other sporting, herding, and working breeds are naturally more athletic than Pugs. Don't expect your Pug to be able to play as vigorously as these breeds.

The Joys of Walking Your Pug

I really enjoy walking my dogs. It is, without question, my favorite activity with them, other than perhaps rubbing their tummies! When I walk my dogs, I'm outside, getting some exercise, and can enjoy my dogs' companionship. I can watch the birds flying over and enjoy the wonderful California sunshine. When I walk along the beach, I can watch the waves breaking on the sand and smell the crisp salt air.

Discover the joys of walking your Pug.

I can learn a lot about my dogs by simply watching their reactions to the world around them while we're walking. Dax and Riker (and now my new puppy Bashir) are very observant and rarely miss anything going on around us. Dax pays more attention to people, while Riker likes to watch birds, rabbits, squirrels, and other critters we encounter. Riker gets really frustrated because the squirrels chirp at him and I won't allow him to chase them. Sometimes we almost have a game going to see who is going to see a squirrel first, Riker or me.

Walking a dog is also a great social activity. Very few people will walk past a Pug without smiling or stopping to say "Hi." Walking any dog is a great icebreaker, but very few people can resist a Pug's appealing features and charming personality.

When a new neighbor moved into our neighborhood and seemed lonely, I asked her if she liked dogs. When she said she had just lost her old dog a few months before she moved, I asked if she was ready for a new one. She adopted a rescue Pug and has finally met almost all her neighbors, just by getting out and walking her new dog.

Walking your Pug will be much more enjoyable when he can walk nicely on leash without pulling. (I'll discuss training tools, including leashes and collars, in Chapter 14 and explain how to train your Pug to walk nicely on leash in Chapter 15.)

Watch Out!

Begin your walking program slowly. Your Pug needs to toughen up both his muscles and the pads of his feet.

The Least You Need to Know

- Making time to play with your Pug is important for the relationship you're building with your dog.

- Play and games are good for your Pug—and for you.

- Although Pugs are not as athletic as many other dog breeds, exercise is still important for good health.

- Never underestimate the joys of walking your Pug.

Part  3

The Healthy Pug

Pugs need regular grooming to keep that short coat clean and shiny. Routine brushing also helps keep shedding under control, thereby keeping the hair in the house to a minimum. Plus, those cute wrinkles on the face need cleaning to keep the skin healthy.

Good nutrition is vital for a healthy dog, so we'll look at dog foods and how the foods your Pug eats affects his health. Part 3 will also look at other health concerns, from working with your veterinarian to spaying and neutering, to potential health threats Pugs face.

The last chapter in this part is one you will want to mark with a bookmark and keep handy; it's a quick reference on emergency first aid for Pugs. Here you'll find life-saving information, including canine CPR, and pointers on how to know when to call the vet.

Chapter 9

Grooming Your Pug

In This Chapter

- 🏠 Grooming your Pug's short coat
- 🏠 Giving your Pug a pedicure
- 🏠 Caring for your Pug's ears and teeth
- 🏠 Eliminating fleas, ticks, and mites

Many people choose a short-haired breed of dog rather than a breed with a longer coat because they think short-haired dogs don't need grooming. But all dogs need regular grooming, even Pugs, with their short hair.

Pugs are naturally quite clean, but they still need to be bathed and brushed, have their toenails trimmed, and have clean ears and teeth. Their facial wrinkles should be cleaned to prevent skin problems, too.

Regular grooming can help keep your Pug comfortable in his own skin and can prevent some health problems.

The Pug's Short Coat

Many people think every short-haired dog has the same coat, but that's not true. Labrador Retrievers have a short coat, yet their hair is much longer than the Pug's and, in most cases, is more coarse. Rottweilers have a short coat, but their skin and hair are oilier than the Pug's. The Doberman Pinscher's short coat is harder, and when it' shed, it's sharper than the Pug's softer hairs. Every short-haired breed has its own unique coat.

A Wonderful Coat

A healthy Pug will have a wonderful coat. The skin should be supple and unblemished and the coat shiny and smooth. A healthy coat draws your hand to it; you can't help but pet it!

The breed standard (see Chapter 2) calls for a fine, smooth, soft, short, and glossy coat that's neither hard nor woolly. Fawn Pugs usually have a *double coat*, with the outer hairs slightly thicker and firmer than the softer under coat. Black Pugs normally have a *single coat* and lack the softer undercoat. There are exceptions to both of these statements, though. Not all fawns have a double coat, and some blacks have a double coat. The standard makes no statement about specific types of coats in specific colors, so neither is right or wrong. Because Pugs are house-dogs, having an undercoat is not nearly as important as it might be for a dog who is outside working in all kinds of weather.

Pug Speak

A dog with a **double coat** will have an outer coat that's more resistant to weather and an inner coat that provides warmth and insulation. A dog with a **single coat** has only the outer coat and lacks the undercoat.

Short Coats Do Shed

One common misconception people have about dogs with a short coat is that they don't shed. In fact, when talking to dog owners, they often tell me they chose the breed of dog they have because they didn't want dog hair in the house. It's only after the dog's been with them for a while that they find out how wrong they were. Unfortunately, they are then often disappointed, and the dog often suffers for it.

Very few breeds of dogs don't shed. Pugs do shed, and their owners are often amazed at how much hair a small dog can lose without becoming bald. Although the shedding is usually worse in the spring and fall, most Pugs shed a certain amount all year round. Regular grooming can lessen the impact of all that hair, and I'll discuss that shortly, but keep in mind that this is normal for the breed and it's something you need to deal with. After all, the breed's appealing qualities far outweigh the problems associated with shedding.

 Pug Smarts

You can lessen some of the impact of your Pug's shed hair on your wardrobe by dressing to match your dog. If you have a black Pug, wear dark colors; if you have a fawn Pug, wear matching clothes.

Stress can also cause a temporary bout of intense shedding. An injury (such as a cut, a pulled muscle, or a fall), a traumatic event (such as an attack by another dog), or even a lengthy car ride if the dog isn't used to traveling can all trigger shedding. One of my dogs begins shedding as soon as she walks into the veterinarian's office. This temporary shedding shouldn't cause you any concern as long as it's short-term. If it lasts more than a few days after the initial stress-causing incident, you might want to talk to your veterinarian.

Health concerns can cause an increase in shedding as well. An illness, anesthesia, or some medications can cause your Pug to shed more than normal. Nutrition also plays a part in a healthy coat, and I'll talk about that more in the next chapter.

You can lessen the impact of shedding by brushing your Pug regularly. Brushing will loosen and pull out the dead hairs, which you can then dispose of after your grooming session rather than picking them off your clothes or vacuuming them off the furniture.

Grooming a Short Coat

Grooming a short coat doesn't require a great deal of your time or energy, but it does need to be done regularly. Your Pug should be brushed every single day, and his facial wrinkles should be cleaned after every meal and after he comes inside from playing in the dirt or grass.

Many Pug owners bathe their dog once a week; I bathe my dogs when they need it. I use the sniff test—if they smell dirty, they get a bath. My dogs are also therapy dogs, so they get a bath prior to each therapy dog visit, too. Other grooming chores, such as toenail-trimming and ear-cleaning, can be done weekly.

Grooming Tools

You won't need many grooming tools to keep your Pug looking his best, but here are a few things to have on hand:

- **A bristle brush.** This can be a natural bristle brush made for people. Most groomers avoid the brushes with nylon bristles, as these can scratch the dog's skin.

- **Shampoo and conditioner.** Choose a mild formula that's safe for puppies and adults and is made for short-haired dogs. Pugs don't need a heavy conditioner formulated for dogs with a long coat that might mat or tangle. Please don't use a shampoo made for humans on your Pug. It will dry out your Pug's skin.

- **Toenail clippers.** Most people find the scissors type easy to use.

- **Antibacterial wipes.** Antibacterial wipes with aloe vera are wonderful for cleaning your Pug's ears and facial wrinkles.

These are the basics. If fleas are a problem in your area, you might want to pick up a *flea comb* as well. If you need help grooming your Pug, talk to your local groomer. He or she might recommend some other tools or products.

Pug Speak

A **flea comb** is a fine-tooth comb that can catch any fleas hiding in the hair.

Brushing and Combing

Professional groomers brush, comb, and clip their clients on a grooming table. By having the dogs off the floor, there's less stress on the groomer's back and the dogs are more likely to stand still and not try to dash away. The dog is more restrained on the table. Many grooming tables even have a leash hook-up to keep the dog still.

You will, like your groomer, want to teach your Pug to stand still on a table while you groom him. You don't need to invest in a professional grooming table; you can use the backyard picnic table, a sturdy folding table, or even the washing machine with the lid down. Don't use the dining room or kitchen table, though! You don't want your Pug to think he's allowed on those tables, or he'll be up there stealing food.

Put a towel or a rubber-backed throw rug on the table to give your Pug some footing so he won't slide. To teach him that standing on the table is good, lift him up and ask him to stand. Help him stand by putting one hand under his belly to position him. Pet him with the other hand, tell him what a good dog he is, feed him a treat, then lift him down. Praise him again. Repeat this several times. If he tries to jump down, squirms, or fights you, use your voice to correct him, "No! Be still!" and

Pug Smarts

You can also use the "Stand" command when your Pug goes to the veterinarian's office. When your Pug will stand nicely on the examination table, the vet can do his or her job much easier.

reposition him. As soon as he cooperates, praise him, "Good boy! Yeah!"

When your Pug will still stand on the table, begin brushing him. Using a soft bristle brush, begin brushing his coat in the direction it grows, starting at the head and working down his body. Gently brush the entire dog, even under his belly and on his tail. Be careful around his eyes.

As you brush, talk softly to your dog and praise him for being good. If he begins to squirm, fight you, or tries to bite you or the brush, stop him and use your voice to let him know he's made a mistake, "No! That's enough!"

Bet You Didn't Know

Some dogs are ticklish and will protest grooming over their tickle spots. Gently but firmly (so you don't tickle) rub those areas with your fingers so your dog learns that even those ticklish spots must be groomed. When you can touch those spots without your Pug squirming, then brush them.

If fleas are a problem in your area, follow up the brushing by running a flea comb through your Pug's coat. Fleas are most apt to hide in the hair on the dog's head, around his tail, in his armpits, and around his genitals. If the flea comb picks up any fleas, drop them in some rubbing alcohol to kill them. (I'll discuss flea control later in this chapter.)

As you brush your Pug, pay attention to his body under his coat. Check for fleas and ticks, cuts or scratches, and lumps and bumps. When you brush your Pug daily and check for potential health threats at the same time, you can catch those problems before they turn into something bigger.

Cleaning Your Pug's Face and Wrinkles

Those adorable wrinkles on your Pug's face can be horrible dirt catchers. When your Pug goes outside to play and sniffs for gophers or rolls in the grass, dust, dirt, blades of grass, grass seeds, and innumerable other bits and pieces of stuff can become caught in his face wrinkles. If the wrinkles aren't cleaned out, sores can fester and his skin could become infected.

You can use a damp cotton ball or a soft washcloth to clean the wrinkles. Many Pug owners have also discovered that the antibacterial wipes suitable for babies and young children also work very well for Pugs' faces. The antibacterial wipes with aloe vera seem to work especially well at keeping the skin clean and healthy.

Gently wipe out each wrinkle on your Pug's face. Be sure you use a clean side of the washcloth or a clean part of the wipe for each wrinkle; you don't want to drag dirt from one wrinkle into another. Sometimes it's easier to clean the wrinkle if you gently open it with one hand as you wipe with the other. Experienced Pug owners can wipe down a Pug's face in a heartbeat, but if you're new at Pug ownership and face-washing, don't worry. You'll get better at it as you practice.

Your Pug's eyelids need regular cleaning, as do the wrinkles around his eyes.

As you clean your Pug's wrinkles, you can also wipe the rest of his face. Gently wipe around his nose and mouth, his chin, and his eyes. His entire face and all his wrinkles and crevasses should be cleaned daily or as often as needed.

Rub-a-Dub-Dub

Always brush your Pug before you bathe him. As you brush him, you might find that he's gotten into something. Here are some suggestions for some grooming challenges:

- **Burrs, foxtails, and other grass seeds.** These can usually be picked out of his coat with your fingers. Unfortunately, many dried grass seeds are the same color as fawn Pugs and can be easily missed. If any remain in his coat, they can work into the skin and cause a serious wound.

- **Oil.** Joy dishwashing soap will cut most oils and greases. Just be sure you rinse out the soap well.

- **Paints and craft colorings.** Most paint solvents are toxic, so don't use them around your Pug. If the paint or craft coloring won't come out with soap and water, carefully use round-tipped scissors to trim it out of the coat.

- **Gum and other sticky stuff.** Use an ice cube to freeze the gum or sticky stuff, then break it out of the coat. If that doesn't work, use a coat conditioner or vegetable oil to ooze it out. If that doesn't work, trim it out of the coat with round-nose scissors.

Pug Smarts

If your Pug comes up with something unusual in his coat and you're not sure how to handle it, call your dog groomer for help.

Always get as much of the trouble stuff out of your Pug's coat as possible prior to getting him wet. If you leave a foreign substance in the coat, it might just spread when you get him wet, and grass seeds, for example, might be harder to find when your dog's wet and covered with shampoo.

When your Pug is brushed and free from all foreign objects, you're ready to bathe him. Pug puppies can be washed in the sink, but most adults are too big and should be bathed in the tub.

Before you put your Pug in the sink or tub, have a couple towels ready, as well as the dog shampoo and conditioner. You don't want to have to go dashing for something and risk having your dog jump out of the sink or tub and hurt himself.

After you have everything ready, put your Pug in the sink or tub. Put a cotton ball in each ear to help keep the water out. Using warm (but not hot) water, thoroughly wet your dog. Shield his eyes as you get his head wet; the water won't hurt his eyes, but it's uncomfortable and will make him dislike his bath. Talk to your dog as you do this, telling him what a good dog he is.

After he's wet, turn off the water and begin working the shampoo into his coat. Again, be careful around his eyes. When he is thoroughly soaped, rinse the soap out of his coat. When the shampoo's rinsed out and you've checked all over to be sure no more shampoo is on him, apply the coat conditioner, following the manufacturer's directions. Then rinse that off, too.

When your Pug is completely rinsed clean, towel him off and wrap him in a towel for a few minutes. Cuddle him while the towel absorbs any remaining moisture and he warms up.

After the Bath

If the weather is warm or your house is well heated, you can let your Pug air dry. However, if the house is chilly, blow dry your dog.

Pug Smarts

When you introduce the blow dryer, have some really good treats at hand. Turn the dryer on the lowest setting and let it blow at the floor close to—but not on—your dog. Praise your Pug and give him a treat. Keep doing this until he's ignoring the blow dryer.

Most dogs dislike the blow dryer because it's too loud and blows a strong wind at them. If you introduce the blow dyer slowly (before you bathe your dog) and feed him treats as you praise him for tolerating the blow dryer, then it won't be so scary when you need to use it to dry him.

As you dry your Pug, either with the towel or the blow dryer, check to be sure all his facial wrinkles are dry, too, and there's no leftover soap or conditioner in them. Then take the cotton out of his ears and check to see that they're dry.

All Those Loose Hairs

When your Pug is dry, brush him again. The bath will have loosened some more dead coat, and if you don't brush it out, it'll end up on the floor and the furniture.

You can live with a dog who sheds. Here are some tips for dealing with the fur:

- Get a good vacuum cleaner. One with a handheld attachment is good. Vacuum daily to get all the hairs off the floor and furniture.

- Use throws or blankets on the furniture to protect against an onslaught of hair as well as the dogs' toenails. Just be sure you choose something that can be thrown in the washing machine and dryer. I use washable blankets, but I also like to use small throw rugs. The rubber backing helps keep them in place so they don't slide, and they're washable.

Pug Smarts

Keep a sticky-tape lint roller in your car so you can go over your clothes before you go into work or to a meeting.

- I am also a big fan of sticky-tape lint rollers to pick up dog hair off my clothes as well as anywhere else I find it. If one

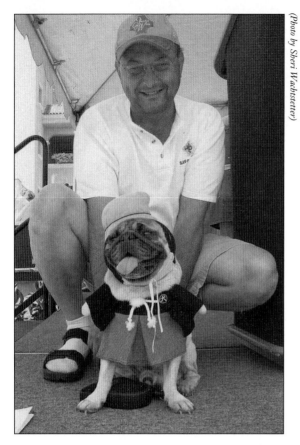

A well-behaved Pug is a great friend and companion.

There's nothing cuter than a Pug's wide-eyed expression of happiness.

A healthy Pug is bright-eyed, alert, and curious about the world around him.

Pugs are social dogs, comfortable with people as well as other dogs.

Gordan, owned by Buddy and Sheri Wachtstetter, is a certified therapy dog.

Pugs can be dignified but can also be clowns. They love to make people laugh.

Before dressing up your Pug, teach him that wearing costumes is fun, not a punishment.

(Photo by Sheri Wachstetter)

Kids, Pugs, and costumes just seem to go together.

(Photo by Jamie Adams)

Black Pugs have a certain appeal all their own.

Pugs will wear costumes, and most seem to like dressing up.

(Photo by Sheri Wachsstetter)

Pugs have a wonderful sense of humor.

Be careful! Pugs are contagious—it's hard to have just one!

Pugs are great dogs, but the breed is not right for everyone. Get to know a Pug or two before adding one to your family.

of the dogs was on the sofa and left a pile of hair behind, I'll grab the tape roller and pick up the hair before it spreads all over the living room.

When you live with a dog (or dogs) who sheds, you have to have a sense of humor. Hair is going to get everywhere, and you just can't get excited about it.

Trimming Your Pug's Toenails

I've heard many experienced Pug owners say that Pugs protest so much when they have their toenails trimmed because they have very sensitive paws. I have yet to see any evidence of extra sensitivity, though. If their paws were sensitive, Pugs would have difficulty walking on different surfaces or climbing agility obstacles. I have seen some very smart Pugs who've taught their owners that they don't like having their nails trimmed!

Very few dogs enjoy having their nails trimmed, and many will protest by barking, whining, wiggling, fighting, and hiding whenever the nail trimmers are in sight. But it doesn't have to be like this. Toenail trimming should be a part of your regular grooming routine (at least weekly) and should be done calmly and gently.

Have your Pug lie down on the table where you do his grooming or on your lap. Take one paw in your hand. Push all the hairs away from the nail so you won't pull any as you trim. The nail is slightly curved over the quick, but it becomes more slender past the quick and curves more sharply. You can see where the quick ends under the nail. The underside of the nail under the quick will be almost flat. Past the quick, the underside of the nail looks almost hollow. Trim the nail slightly beyond the quick. It will hurt your Pug if you cut the quick, so try not to!

 Pug Smarts

If you cut the quick and the nail bleeds, scrape the nail along a bar of soap. The soap will clog the nail until a clot forms.

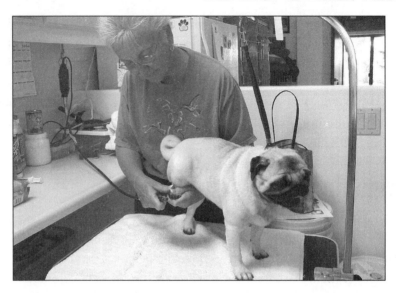

Keep toenail trimming calm and gentle; don't let it escalate into a fight.

If your Pug has had some bad nail-trimming experiences, just trim the nails on one paw at a time. Do the left front one day and the right front the next day. Take four days to do his nails if you need to. If you try to do all four feet at once, the grooming session could turn into a horrible experience for the both of you.

Pug Smarts

A good way to distract your Pug while you trim his nails is to give him a spoonful of peanut butter. It will stick to the roof of his mouth, and he'll be so interested in eating it, he'll forget what you're doing to his toes!

If you feel really uncomfortable trimming your Pug's nails, most groomers will trim the nails for a very reasonable cost. If you have your groomer do it, plan on visiting regularly; every other week is best. Nails grow very quickly, and too-long nails will hurt your Pug's feet.

You Pug's Ears, Teeth, and More

There's more to grooming your Pug than cleaning his wrinkles, brushing and bathing his coat, and trimming his toenails. You also need to keep his ears clean, brush his teeth, and check his anal glands. Although these are no one's favorite chores, they are necessary. Once you make doing them a habit, they aren't as bad as they sound at first.

Cleaning Your Pug's Ears

To clean your Pug's ears, you'll need a few cotton balls and some witch hazel or a commercial ear-cleaning solution. You can also use antibacterial wipes with aloe vera.

Dip the cotton ball in witch hazel and then squeeze out the excess. You want the cotton ball damp but not wet. Using the damp cotton ball or a wipe, gently hold the ear flap so the ear is accessible and begin wiping the inside of the ear. Get into all the folds and creases. Don't go deep inside the ear; just clean what is easily reachable. If the ear is dirty, use two or three cotton balls or wipes.

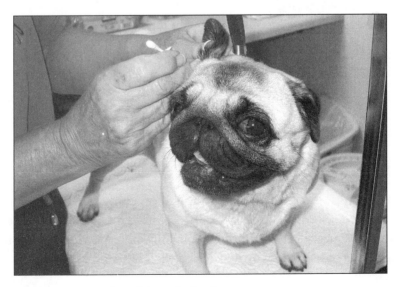

Your Pug's ears need careful, gentle cleaning.

Cleaning Your Pug's Teeth

Dirty teeth cause more than just bad breath; they can also lead to major health problems, including heart disease. Bacteria from a dirty mouth can also affect the dog's liver and kidneys, often quite seriously.

You can clean your Pug's teeth by using a small child's toothbrush or by wrapping your index finger with gauze. Use a small amount of baking soda or a toothpaste made for dogs, and rub the teeth and gums.

Very few dogs enjoy having their teeth brushed, but most will learn to accept it. Just start gradually, doing a small part of the dog's mouth and then stopping. Come back later (or the next day) and do a little more. Don't try to do all your Pug's teeth at once; he will fight you. As he becomes more accepting, you can do more each time.

Watch Out!

Don't use toothpaste made for people on your pugs. Not all human products are safe for dogs, and most dogs dislike the minty taste.

Many Pugs have crowded or crooked teeth. Be sure to get these teeth very clean so they don't cause problems later. Get the toothbrush bristles between the teeth, really working the toothpaste or baking soda in there. You can even use a piece of gauze to floss between the teeth. Then just let the dog drink water to rinse.

What Are Anal Glands?

The anal glands are small glands located on either side of the anus. As the dog relieves himself, a small amount of oil produced by the glands is squeezed out with the feces. This oil is individual to each dog and is one reason why dogs smell each other's feces and rear ends.

When a dog's feces are habitually soft or when the glands produce too much oil, the glands will become full, causing pressure and irritation for your dog. Many dogs will try to relieve this irritation by dragging their rear end on the ground, trying to scrape the anal glands. Unfortunately, this can get dirt into the anal glands, causing even more irritation, sometimes to the point of serious infection.

Groomers often routinely express (empty) anal glands during grooming, especially if a particular dog is known to have a problem. However, because many dogs express their anal glands themselves, this shouldn't be done unless your veterinarian recommends it. During your Pug's next vet visit, ask your vet if this needs to be done.

Fleas, Ticks, and Other Bugs

Fleas, ticks, and mites are external parasites uniquely suited to pester your Pug. They bite your dog, suck his blood, and can transmit a whole menu of diseases. But that's not all—they've reaked havoc throughout the world for as long as we have kept any kind of record. Fleas have been blamed for innumerable plagues throughout history, including the bubonic plague that ravaged Europe many centuries ago. And these pests can still cause problems for both you and your Pug.

Fleas

A flea is a tiny, crescent-shaped insect with a big abdomen and a small head. It has six legs and is a tremendous jumper. It's very skinny and flat sided so it can slide through your dog's hair with ease.

Fleas live by biting your dog, taking a drop of blood each time they bite. A heavy infestation can actually cause anemia in a Pug.

Watch Out!

Fleas are also the intermediate host for tapeworms, so dogs with fleas should also be checked for tapeworms.

Many dogs are so allergic to the flea's saliva, they bite and chew each flea bite wound, causing even more irritation and damage. An allergic dog can end up with flea-bite dermatitis or open sores, which can then lead to secondary infections.

In the past, controlling fleas meant the dog, yard, and house all needed to be treated with potentially toxic insecticides, exposing both the dog and the family. Flea control is much easier these days, thanks to several products:

- **Systemic topical treatments.** These products are applied to the skin, usually between the dog's shoulder blades. The product is absorbed through the skin into the dog's system. Depending on the product, either the flea is killed when it bites the dog or its reproductive cycle is disrupted.

- **Systemic products.** Your dog swallows a pill, which transmits a chemical throughout his bloodstream. When a flea bites him, it picks up this chemical, which then prevents the flea's eggs from developing.

- **Insect growth regulators.** These products stop the immature flea from developing or maturing, thereby stopping reproduction.

Watch Out!
Always read the directions on flea products and follow them to the letter. Incorrect use could cause great harm to you, your family, or your Pug.

New products are constantly being introduced, so talk to your veterinarian to find out what he or she recommends for your Pug.

Ticks

Ticks are eight-legged, oblong insects with a head that embeds into your dog's skin. Ticks feed on blood, and when engorged, they'll drop off. Ticks, like fleas, can also carry disease. In the United

States, ticks can carry Rocky Mountain Spotted Fever and Lyme disease as well as other potentially serious diseases.

Although some flea products are partially effective in killing ticks, they are rarely effective at repelling them. During tick season (which, depending on where you live, can be spring, summer, and/or fall), you'll have to examine your dog every day and remove each and every tick. Pay particular attention to your dog's neck, behind his ears, his armpits, and his groin area.

Never remove a tick with your bare fingers. If it's carrying a disease and you have any break in your skin or you then touch your face, you could infect yourself. Instead, wear gloves or use tweezers or forceps to remove the tick. Grab the tick close to the skin and gently pull it out. Don't yank it, though. You might leave the head in the skin, which could lead to an infection. Put a little antibiotic ointment on your dog's skin where you pulled off the tick.

Drop the removed tick in some rubbing alcohol to kill it. Don't flush it down the toilet; it will live to bite another animal later.

Mange Mites

Mange isn't limited to strays or neglected dogs. Many well-loved dogs have come down with mange. Mange is caused by mites (tiny microscopic pests) that live on your dog. There are two varieties:

- *Sarcoptic mange* is contagious to people and other pets. Its primary symptom is red welts, and the dog will be scratching continuously. Sarcoptic mange usually responds well to treatment.

- *Demodectic mange* is not considered contagious and shows up with bald patches, usually on the dog's face first. Your dog might or might not scratch or itch. Demodectic mange usually appears in young dogs, often males, and many times will appear during adolescence. It usually responds well to treatment. However, older dogs with demodectic mange might not respond as well.

Although I've given you a lot of information here, don't let it overwhelm you. Grooming a Pug is not hard. Just establish a routine and stick to it. Your Pug will learn to appreciate the attention, he'll be clean and well cared for, and you'll feel good about your efforts.

The Least You Need to Know

🏠 Pugs have a short coat, but it still needs regular grooming.

🏠 Trim your Pug's toenails weekly and the process won't be so stressful.

🏠 Wash your Pug's face—including his wrinkles. His ears and teeth need regular cleaning, too.

🏠 Fleas, ticks, and mites are horrible pests that can cause your Pug discomfort as well as threaten his health.

10

Filling Your Pug's Tummy

In This Chapter

- 🏠 Canine nutrition—a controversial subject
- 🏠 Evaluating commercial dog foods
- 🏠 Making home-cooked food for your Pug
- 🏠 Taking a look at supplements

The adage said, "You are what you eat," and scientists today agree. It's hard to watch the evening news or read a newspaper or magazine without finding out that we should not eat a certain food or that we should be eating more of something else. We're learning that good food is important for our long-term good health. The same applies to our Pugs, too. What your dog eats is just as important to his long-term good health as it is to ours.

Canine Nutrition

Dogs are *carnivores*, or meat-eaters, just as their ancient ancestors and distant cousins, the wolves and coyotes, are. They might catch their prey, or they might take advantage of finding carrion

Pug Speak

A **carnivore** eats meat; an **omnivore** eats plants and meat; and an **herbivore** eats only plants.

(already-dead prey). Very few canine carnivores limit themselves only to meat, though. Most will also eat fallen fruits, berries, and some tubers and roots. Although behaviorally most canines are, therefore, *omnivores*, scientifically they are classified as carnivores.

Our Pugs today obviously do not and cannot hunt their own dinner. They are entirely too domesticated, and their body size and jaw structure would make them very inefficient hunters. In addition, very few Pug owners would be happy seeing their treasured pet bringing in a rabbit from the backyard or neighboring field.

It's up to us, then, to be sure our Pugs eat the very best diet possible to fulfill their nutritional needs. Good nutrition helps the body function as it should, maintains the dog's health, and enables him to grow. Good nutrition also provides energy for work, exercise, and play.

Good nutrition is made up of many things:

- **Vitamins.** These organic compounds are necessary for life. Without them, food would not be digested, the dog could not grow, and a thousand other bodily functions would stop. Several vitamins, including A, D, E, and K, are fat soluble, which means the body can store them for future use. Other vitamins, including all the B complex vitamins and C, are water soluble and must be provided in each day's diet.

- **Minerals.** Minerals are inorganic compounds, and although they're necessary for life, they're needed in much smaller quantities than vitamins. Necessary minerals include calcium, phosphorus, copper, iron, and potassium, as well as several others. Minerals are required in a delicate balance for good health, and more is not necessarily better. Most minerals work only in the presence of either other minerals or vitamins.

Protein. Meat is good-quality protein for dogs and can be found in beef, chicken, lamb, fish, or any other meat. Proteins can be found in other sources, too, including eggs and dairy products. Some proteins can be found in plants and/or plant products, including tofu, which is made from soybeans. Complete proteins contain all the amino acids necessary for good health. Good sources of complete proteins include eggs, red meats, fish, milk, and dairy products. Incomplete proteins contain some but not all the needed amino acids. Sources of incomplete proteins include beans, soybeans, peanuts, grains, and potatoes.

Amino acids. Amino acids are necessary for many body functions, including growth and healing as well as for hormone, antibody, and enzyme production. When proteins are digested, they're broken down into amino acids, making them usable by the body. There are 22 known amino acids; 12 of those—arginine, citrulline, histidine, isoleucine, leucine, lysine, methionine, phenylalanine, taurine, threonine, tryptophan, and valine—are necessary for canine life.

Enzymes. Enzymes are protein-based chemicals that cause biochemical reactions in the body. These reactions affect every stage of *metabolism*. Some enzymes must work with a partner, a coenzyme that is often a vitamin, to cause the needed reaction. Some enzymes are produced by the dog's body, and others are found in the food the dog eats.

Pug Speak
Metabolism is the body process of breaking down food to its chemical parts, which can then be used by the body.

Fats. Although fats have gotten a bad name lately, they are a necessary part of good nutrition, especially for growing puppies and active dogs. Fats are needed to metabolize the fat-soluble

Bet You Didn't Know

Some dogs who are fed diets (or commercial foods) high in carbohydrates, especially carbohydrates from cereal grains, show symptoms of hyperactivity. These symptoms often disappear when the dog is fed a diet higher in animal protein and lower in cereal grain carbohydrates.

vitamins and supply energy for activity. Fats can be found in animal meats and in plant-based oils.

🐾 **Carbohydrates.** Carbohydrates are sugars and starches found in plants and are used in the body as fuel. Complex carbohydrates such as potatoes and grains are intricate conglomerations of glucose (sugar) molecules.

Good food is a tool to help keep your Pug strong and healthy.

Commercial Dog Foods

Dog owners need to remember that commercial pet foods are a multibillion-dollar business, and pet food manufacturers are in the business to make a profit. Although many commercial dog foods are good foods, dog owners should watch all those flashy commercials and advertisements with a good dose of skepticism.

All Dog Foods Are Not Created Equal

What makes one commercial dog food better than another can be based on many things. One factor to consider is how the food is tested during development. Testing might consist of *feeding trials*, and in fact, many of the larger dog food companies maintain large kennels for feeding trials. But not all feeding trials are equal. Some dog food companies will feed generations of dogs their foods for long-term trials, while other feeding trials might be a much shorter period of time (some as little as 6 months in length).

Pug Speak

Feeding trials are tests in which a certain number of dogs are fed a specific food, and only that food, in a controlled environment such as a kennel. The dogs' health is analyzed during and after the trial period.

Some companies use laboratory testing to determine the nutritional value of a dog food. However, laboratory testing doesn't necessarily prove that a dog will thrive on the food. Years ago, a dog food manufacturer tested a variety of strange "ingredients" (including an old leather boot, a quart of motor oil, and a few other odd items) and found they contained a list of proteins, fats, and other necessary dietary requirements that could feed a dog. On paper, the necessary dietary requirements were met; in actuality, the dog would not have survived. Obviously, both feeding trials and laboratory testing have their positive aspects and negative drawbacks.

The quality of the food is also based on the quality of the ingredients. Grains grown in mineral-poor soils will have few minerals to pass along to the dog. Poor-quality meats will be less nourishing to the dog. Some dog foods will supply needed nutrition by

Bet You Didn't Know

Pugs suffering from poor nutrition will have a dull coat that sheds excessively, flaky skin, brittle toenails, and no energy for extended work or play.

adding artificial supplements rather than relying on quality ingredients to supply the nutrition.

Do you remember the adage, "You get what you pay for"? Although it's not 100 percent true (nothing ever is, is it?), dog foods are one of those things where most of the time you do get what you pay for. The less expensive the dog food, the cheaper the ingredients in it.

Reading the Labels

The label on the dog food bag will tell you a lot about the food inside. One section of the label lists the percentages of nutrients. Most Pugs will thrive on a food that contains between 26 and 28 percent protein and 8 percent fat. The labels rarely tell you how much of the food is carbohydrates, although many of the major dog food manufacturers do have a page on their website with more detailed food information, including carbohydrate percentages.

The label will also list the food ingredients in order of the amounts contained. If beef is listed first, followed by rice, corn, and wheat, you know there's more beef in the food than rice, and there's more rice than corn. This can be deceptive, though. For example, a label lists the following ingredients: beef, wheat bran, wheat germ, and wheat midlings. Does that mean there's more beef than wheat? No, it doesn't. It just means there's more beef than each one of the other individual ingredients. When all the wheat ingredients are added together, there could very well be much more wheat than beef.

 Pug Smarts

Pugs can be very prone to food allergies. Your vet might recommend allergy tests; this is a good idea. Then you'll know exactly what your Pug is allergic to and can avoid those ingredients by reading the dog food labels.

Reading the labels on your Pug's food can help you avoid foods that you might not want your dog to eat or those foods your Pug might be allergic to. If your dog appears to have a behavioral sensitivity to carbohydrates (it will manifest as hyperactivity), read the labels and choose a food with fewer carbs.

Once you've studied dog food labels and chosen a food you and your dog both like, don't assume it will always remain the same. Foods do change. Sometimes the manufacturers will take advantage of the change by marketing the food as "New!" and "Improved!" but many times they simply change the labels. If your Pug is allergic to some specific ingredients, be sure to read the label each and every time you buy the food.

Are Preservatives Safe?

Preservatives are usually added to dog foods to increase the food's shelf life and to keep it from spoiling. Unfortunately, some preservatives are controversial. The current questionable preservative used in dog foods is ethoxyquin, a chemical that prevents the fats in foods from becoming rancid. It also helps vitamins retain their potency. Ethoxyquin has been approved by the Food and Drug Administration (FDA) for use in human foods, but it has come under criticism from the general public. It's been alleged that ethoxyquin causes cancer and kidney, liver, and thyroid problems. Although none of these claims have been proven, you, as your dog's owner and feeder, can certainly avoid these foods if you're concerned.

If you're concerned about any dog food preservatives, look for one preserved with tocopherols. These antioxidants are naturally occurring compounds of vitamins C and E. Be mindful of the food's expiration date, though. Tocopherols have a short shelf life.

Types of Dog Foods

For many years, dogs ate what their owners ate—usually the table leftovers. When commercial dog foods were introduced, the two basic forms were dry kibble and canned foods. Today, there are also semi-moist foods, fresh foods, frozen foods, and dehydrated foods—a banquet of choices!

🏠 **Dry kibble dog foods** come in a bag and have a reasonably long shelf life, depending on what preservatives are used. Most of these foods contain grains and meats and are usually quite affordable, especially when compared to other types of dog foods.

Pug Smarts

Small dogs, especially those with less than the best teeth, can have trouble chewing large-size dry kibble. If you want to feed your Pug kibble, choose a food with smaller kibbles, or crush them prior to feeding.

🏠 **Canned dog foods** are mostly meats or meat recipes (processed meats with other ingredients). These foods have a high moisture content. In the can, they have a long shelf life, but when the can is opened, the food must be used right away. Canned foods are very palatable to dogs and are much more expensive than dry foods.

🏠 **Semi-moist foods** have a higher moisture content than dry food but not as high as canned foods. These foods are very high in sugar and salt as well as artificial colorings. The ingredients can vary significantly, so read the labels on these foods very carefully. Many dog treats are semi-moist because the sugar and salt ingredients make these very attractive to dogs.

🏠 **Fresh foods** have become quite popular recently. These foods usually have a meat base and might have vegetables and fruits added. Fresh foods generally don't use cereal grains but instead use sweet potatoes, apples, bananas, or other noncereal grain foods. Fresh foods are very difficult to keep without adding preservatives, so the shelf life is a matter of days. Many fresh foods are frozen and must be thawed prior to serving.

🏠 **Dehydrated foods** have been essentials for campers, backpackers, and hikers for many years. There were very few good dehydrated dog foods, though, until recently. The demand for quality dog foods has stimulated the market, and today there are several good-quality dehydrated foods. Dehydrated foods are made from meats, vegetables, and fruits. Some include cereal grains, while others do not. You simply re-hydrate these foods with warm water prior to serving.

🏠 Some Pug owners prefer to feed **human foods** to their dog, preparing their dog's food on a regular basis rather than feeding a commercial food (see the following "Making Your Pug's Food" section).

Pugs don't eat very much, especially compared to the amount of food a larger dog will eat. Therefore, choosing the right food is very important, not just for your peace of mind but also for your Pug's long-term health.

Looking at Supplements

Many people take vitamins because taking one provides some nutrients they don't get from their diet and gives them a feeling of security regarding their own diet. For the same reason, some dog owners feel better when they give their dog a vitamin *supplement*.

Supplements don't have to be in pill form, however. A supplement is anything that's added to the basic diet (yours or your dog's) and can include vitamin pills,

Pug Speak

A **supplement** is anything that is added to the basic diet and can include foods, pills, and herbal remedies.

foods, and herbal remedies. A supplement can sometimes make the difference between an adequate diet and a much better one.

Natural Foods

Although many people feel that the best source of vitamins and minerals is delivered in pill form, don't forget that the original source of these nutrients is from food. Many nutritional experts for both people and dogs still recommend basic foods as the best and most complete sources of essential nutrients.

Some food supplements that can be added to your Pug's diet can include the following:

- 🏠 **Yogurt.** A good, nutritious food in its own right, yogurt is a good source of protein, amino acids, and fat. Yogurt with live active cultures adds beneficial bacteria to the digestive tract. Add no more than 1 teaspoon per day for a Pug.

- 🏠 **Brewer's yeast.** An excellent source of B vitamins, brewer's yeast also contains several minerals, including selenium and chromium. A dash or a pinch per day is great for a Pug.

- 🏠 **Eggs.** Eggs have often been called the perfect food, as they are wonderful sources of amino acids, enzymes, and protein. Feed your Pug only cooked eggs, because raw egg yolks interfere with vitamin B absorption. Raw eggs have also been associated with salmonella poisonings. Cook 1 egg, shell it, crumble the egg, and split it up among several meals.

- 🏠 **Kelp.** Kelp is a good source of several minerals, including iodine, calcium, potassium, and other minerals. Use according to manufacturer's directions (normally a pinch per day is fine for a Pug).

Vitamins

Your Pug needs a good supply of the essential vitamins, which includes A, B complex, C, D, E, and K. If your dog's eating a good-quality commercial food, vitamins are supplied both in the ingredients and as additives to the food itself. Most dog food manufacturers add vitamins because the processing of the ingredients can destroy many vitamins. Do not add additional vitamins to your dog's diet without discussing this with your veterinarian. More vitamins is not better, as the fat-soluble vitamins can be toxic when given in excess.

If you're feeding your dog a diet you've formulated at home, either a home-cooked formula or raw foods, you might want to add a vitamin tablet to your dog's daily diet. This will help make sure your dog gets everything he needs. After all, very few dog owners are canine nutritionists.

Minerals

Commercial dog food manufacturers add minerals to their foods just as they do vitamins. Don't add a mineral supplement to an already balanced commercial food unless you first discuss it with your veterinarian and add the mineral(s) for a very specific reason.

If you're feeding your dog a diet you've formulated at home, you can add a mineral supplement, usually in conjunction with a vitamin supplement, just to be sure he's getting all the essential minerals he needs. Follow the manufacturer's directions for the supplement; do not give extra.

Herbal Remedies

Many dog owners give their dogs a variety of herbal remedies for many different reasons. Some owners want to address some very specific health concerns, as my husband and I are doing with our 10-year-old dog Dak, who has liver disease. Her diet and supplemental herbal remedies are keeping her liver disease in check (see the following "Cooking for Your Pug" section). Other dog owners use herbal remedies as preventive medicine to try to keep the immune system healthy.

Many dog owners don't realize that herbal remedies can be as potent as many prescription medicines and shouldn't be given indiscriminately. Before adding any herbal remedies to your dog's diet, do some research. Appendix B lists a few herbal medicine sources, but also talk to your veterinarian. As with any form of medicine—human, canine, or alternative—be sure you aren't going to cause any harm.

Cooking for Your Pug

I cook for one of my dogs, Dak. She's now 10 years old and is suffering from congenital liver disease. An incorrect diet can stress the liver, so I've been feeding her a home-cooked diet (with her veterinarian's approval) for several years, and we've been able to keep her liver stable. The home-cooked diet won't cure her liver disease, but it has helped keep the disease from progressing as rapidly as it was prior to changing her diet. In addition, at 10 years of age, she is still eager to play, does her obedience training, and enjoys her agility. Her coat is shiny and healthy, and her eyes are showing her age (slightly cloudy) but still bright and aware. For Dax, this diet is the right choice.

But feeding a homemade diet can be a lot of work. It's certainly much more work than scooping some dry kibble out of a bag and dumping it in a bowl. Feeding a homemade diet also requires thought and research, because it can be quite difficult to formulate a homemade diet that meets all your Pug's nutritional needs. Because Pugs are small and have a small stomach, they can be a special challenge to cook for. It's hard to feed a very small meal and be sure everything your Pug needs is in that small amount of food.

I've found that to make the homemade diet work, it's important to use a variety of ingredients to be sure the dog is receiving all the necessary amino acids, enzymes, vitamins, and minerals. Any diet that emphasizes one ingredient too much can potentially lead to a nutritional deficiency.

Cooked or Raw?

Dog owners who cook for their dogs do so for the same reasons they cook their own foods. Cooking brings out the flavor of many foods and begins to break down the food so it's more easily consumed and digested. Cooking also makes many foods safer, killing bacteria that could cause illnesses.

Because the early dogs and wild canines eat only raw foods, there's a movement today that encourages dog owners to feed their dogs raw foods as well, including raw meats (plus the bones), vegetables, and fruits. Advocates state that raw foods are healthier, more natural, and will prolong their dogs' lives.

Although this movement is growing, not all canine experts agree, especially many veterinarians. Most experts worry about the quality of the meat being eaten and the dangers associated with feeding a dog bones. If you're interested in feeding your dog a raw diet, do some research, get as much information (pro and con) as you can, then make an appointment to talk to your veterinarian.

Adding to a Commercial Diet

Some Pug owners would like to feed their dog a better diet than a dry kibble commercial food, yet might not be convinced about the safety of a raw food diet or might find cooking a homemade diet overwhelming. Luckily, there are alternatives:

🏠 Use a good-quality dry kibble dog food as a base, and supplement it with a dehydrated food that's been re-hydrated with warm water.

- Use a good-quality dry kibble as a base, and supplement it with home-cooked meals (see the next sections).

- Use one of the dehydrated foods (re-hydrated with warm water) as a base, and add a few kibbles for texture.

- Use one of the dehydrated foods (re-hydrated with warm water) as a base, and add good-quality raw meat, grated vegetables, and a piece of banana.

As a general rule of thumb, don't add more than 10 percent new food to a commercial food. Any more than that could upset the food's nutritional balance.

Bet You Didn't Know

There are exceptions to every rule, it seems. Force, a dehydrated food made by The Honest Kitchen (www. thehonestkitchen.com) was formulated so additional foods (including raw meat) could be added without adversely affecting the food's nutritional balance.

The Basic Home-Cooked Diet

The following diet is a home-cooked maintenance diet for dogs with no known allergies or sensitivities. The amount you feed each day will vary depending on your Pug's weight, weight loss or gain, activity level, and energy needs. Most Pugs should be offered ½ to ⅔ cup per meal (figuring on 2 meals per day). Increase or decrease the amount fed as your Pug gains or loses weight.

Mix well in a big bowl:

1 lb. cooked ground meat (chicken, turkey, or lamb) drained of most of the fat

2 cups whole cooked millet or amaranth

½ cup cooked, mashed barley

½ cup cooked oatmeal

½ cup grated carrots

½ cup finely chopped green vegetables (no lettuce)

2 TB. olive oil

2 TB. minced or mashed garlic

Divide the mixture into meal-size servings, and store in the freezer. Thaw 1 day's servings at a time. When serving, add the following:

Bet You Didn't Know

When you feed home-cooked meals, pay attention to your Pug's teeth to keep them clean and healthy. Because home-cooked meals are soft, they don't have the teeth-cleaning properties crunching on dry kibble does.

1 tsp. yogurt with live active cultures

1 multi-vitamin/mineral supplement

Tiny pinch kelp

A Special Home-Cooked Diet

The following diet is for dogs recuperating from illness or injury or for pregnant or lactating female dogs. It's also a good diet for dogs under stress, such as Pugs competing in obedience or agility, or those on the show circuit.

Mix together in a large bowl:

1 lb. cooked ground meat, do not drain off the fat

4 large hardboiled eggs, shelled and crumbled

1 cup cooked whole-grain brown rice

1 cup cooked oatmeal

1 large sweet potato, mashed

½ cup grated carrots

½ cup finely chopped green vegetables (no lettuce)

2 TB. olive oil

2 TB. minced or mashed garlic

Divide the mixture into individual servings, and freeze. Thaw 1 day's servings at a time. When serving, add the following:

1 tsp. yogurt with live active cultures

Dash dry powdered milk

Dash brewer's yeast

Pinch kelp

1 multi-vitamin/mineral supplement

A Hypoallergenic Diet

This diet can be adapted to individual dogs, depending on the dog's allergies and sensitivities.

Mix together in a large bowl:

5 large potatoes (russet or sweet potatoes or a mixture of both), cooked and mashed

3 hardboiled eggs, shelled and crumbled

1 cup finely chopped green vegetables (no lettuce)

1 cup cooked beans (not green beans), finely chopped or mashed

½ cup grated carrots

2 TB. olive oil

1 TB. minced garlic

Divide the mixture into individual servings, and freeze. Thaw 1 day's servings at a time. When serving, add:

1 tsp. yogurt with live active cultures

1 multi-vitamin/mineral supplement

Pinch kelp

Note: If your Pug is allergic to dairy products, don't use yogurt. Add an acidophilus supplement instead.

Changing Foods

Pugs can have a delicate digestive system. They might or might not get sick, vomit, or have diarrhea, but they do get quite flatulent when things are not right inside! If you want to change your Pug's diet, do so very gradually over 2 or 3 weeks. Add ¼ of the new food to ¾ of the old food for several days. Then, over the next 2 weeks or so, gradually increase the new food and decrease the old one.

 Watch Out!

If your Pug has an upset stomach, diarrhea, bad gas, or doesn't want to eat, you're probably changing the food too quickly.

Dinnertime!

It's not hard to feed Pugs; they all like to eat. Some breeds tend to be picky or poor eaters, but Pugs don't have this problem. Now, that's not to say they can't be manipulative—they can be! If your Pug learns that if he looks sad or just picks at his food, you'll add some canned dog food, some cheese, or leftovers to his food, he will use that to his advantage.

Your Pug should not be skinny, but he shouldn't be fat, either.

When to Feed?

Most Pugs, puppies and adults, do well when fed twice a day. Decide on a schedule that works for you. Perhaps feeding your Pug breakfast while you eat yours, then feeding him his evening meal after your family has finished dinner works best. He can eat while you clean up the kitchen. The actual timing isn't important.

Once you've established a schedule, stick to it, or your Pug won't be happy.

How Much to Feed?

I am asked this question often, but there's no set answer. Although every dog food manufacturer has a chart stating how much food should be fed according to the dog's size, that rarely applies to Pugs. Pugs gain weight too easily, and if you fed your Pug the amount listed on the dog food bag, he would be a walking watermelon!

Every dog is different, and every dog food is different. You have to feed your Pug, watch him, see whether he gains or loses weight, then make adjustments to the amount you feed.

Stocky Doesn't Mean *Fat!*

When I talked to veterinarians about this book, I asked them about some of the most common problems they saw in Pugs. One of the problems almost every vet mentioned was weight (I'll discuss the other problems in Chapter 12). Too many Pugs are fat.

Watch Out!

Excess weight is just as dangerous for our dogs as it is for us. Don't let your Pug get fat!

Pugs are supposed to be stocky and cobby, yes. But *stocky* doesn't mean *fat!* Pugs should have a little meat over their ribs, but they should also have a defined waist. They should be able to work and play without having to stop every few minutes to catch their breath or because they're too heavy.

Evaluating Your Pug's New Food

When you've decided on a food you and your Pug like, and after your Pug has been eating the food for 4 to 6 weeks, evaluate the results. This is the foods' final test and will help you decide whether you should continue feeding this food or change to something else. Here's what to look for:

- How is your Pug's weight? Pugs are cobby but should not be fat. You should be able to feel ribs (with a little meat over them) but not see them.

- How is your Pug's skin and coat? It should be shiny and soft.

- Does your Pug have the energy to play? Is he lethargic? Is he hyper? He should have the energy for work and play but not be bouncing off the walls.

- Does he chew on inappropriate things? Often dogs lacking something in their diet will chew on things to satisfy that need. They will eat dirt, chew on rocks, the stucco on the side of the house, or wood.

If you have any questions, talk to your veterinarian. Just be aware that not all veterinarians specialize in canine nutrition. You can also talk to the dog food companies. They will try to talk you into buying their foods, of course, but they are usually helpful in regards to the ingredients used, additives, and preservatives.

The Least You Need to Know

- As a general rule, you get what you pay for with dog foods. The more expensive foods are better quality.

- Dog food labels will tell you a lot about the food, including ingredients, nutritional value, and what preservatives are used.

- Healthful, homemade diets are possible, but take care with the ingredients and watch your Pug closely to monitor the results.

- Most Pugs, puppies and adults, do well when fed twice a day.

- Pugs have a tendency to put on weight. Don't let your dog get fat! It's harmful to his health.

11

Keeping Your Pug Healthy with Your Vet's Help

In This Chapter

- 🏠 Working with your Pug's health partner
- 🏠 Understanding the importance and dangers of vaccinations
- 🏠 Spaying and neutering
- 🏠 Breeding Pugs difficulties

For the most part, Pugs are small, sturdy, healthy dogs, but they can't maintain this on their own. Your Pug needs your help to stay healthy, and you, in turn, need a veterinarian's guidance to know what to do for your Pug. Your veterinarian is your Pug's health-care professional; he or she is your Pug's partner in good health.

Your Veterinarian: Your Pug's Health Partner

A veterinarian you trust will be of great help to you in maintaining your Pug's continued good health. In addition, should your Pug face a health threat, working with a veterinarian whose judgment and knowledge you have confidence in will be of tremendous value. Even long-time dog owners and breeders have questions about canine health, and your veterinarian is the person to ask. Your neighbor, friend, or family members might offer help, but they might also give you incorrect or incomplete information.

Bet You Didn't Know

In the text, I refer to the veterinarian as a "he" for simplicity's sake. It's very awkward to write (and read) "he or she." However, by doing so, I mean no disrespect for women veterinarians. Several women veterinarians were interviewed for this book.

In Chapter 4, I discussed finding a veterinarian and how to establish yourself as a client. Now that your Pug is a member of your family, he needs to go meet your veterinarian, too.

Most breeders, shelters, and rescue groups require in their contract that your new dog be examined by a veterinarian within the first few days after joining your family. Be sure you do this. Not only will you get some reassurance that your Pug is healthy, but should there be a health problem, it will be recognized right away and you can then decide whether to keep the dog and deal with the problem, or give it back before you become too attached to the dog.

During the first exam, your vet will look at your Pug's eyes, ears, teeth, mouth, skin, coat, and genitals. He will look at the outside of your Pug for any outward problems and will then examine your Pug with his hands. He will feel for anything out of the ordinary that could indicate potential problems. He will also watch your Pug as he moves his hands over the dog's body to see if the dog tenses or winces when touched. This could signal soreness from rough play, an injury, or an illness.

If your vet is familiar with Pugs (and hopefully you chose him because he is), he will also be looking for congenital problems sometimes found in the breed. (I'll discuss these in more detail in Chapter 12.)

Bet You Didn't Know

Some people seem to resent the money spent at the veterinarian's office. Your vet's goal is your goal, too—to keep your Pug healthy. Any money spent in preventive care is money well spent.

Talking to Your Vet

Your vet can learn a lot about your Pug by examining him, but he is also seeing your dog in an artificial situation. Your Pug is standing on the examination table; he's not running up and down the hallway or chasing your cat. Nor is he sleeping on the sofa or doing any one of a hundred of his normal activities.

During this first visit, and throughout your Pug's life, talk to your vet about your Pug, especially if you have any concerns. Tell him about the wince you saw when you were brushing him the day before or the yelp you heard when he was chasing the birds in the backyard. Tell him about your Pug's appetite, his stools, and how much he sleeps. The more information you can give your vet, the better. Don't try to decide yourself what's important and what isn't; just explain as much as you can, and your vet will wade through the information.

If you must take your Pug to the vet's office because of a problem, ask yourself some questions and make some notes so you have all the information he might need:

🏠 Take a look at your Pug's stools. Do they look normal? If not, what's different? Bring a small sample to the vet's office so they can be analyzed.

🏠 Does your Pug have difficulty urinating? Does the urine look normal? If not, what's different? Color? Smell?

🏠 How is your Pug's appetite? Does he act hungry before he eats? Does he eat all of his meal? Does he vomit before or after eating? Did he eat anything out of the ordinary?

🏠 Does your Pug appear to hurt anywhere?

🏠 Has his activity level changed? Is he refusing to work, train, exercise, or play? What is he doing (or not doing) specifically?

🏠 Has his attitude changed? Is he clingy or grumpy? Has he shown some fear or aggression? Has he had some housetraining accidents?

Take all this information with you to your appointment with the vet and offer all of it to him. He can decide what's most important and use that to find out what's wrong.

Listening to Your Vet

Just as you should talk to your vet and he should listen to the information you have for him, you should also listen to your vet. Bring some paper and a pen to the appointment if you need to, and take notes. Many people are flustered in the veterinarian's office and, once home, can't remember what was said. Your Pug's health might depend on your ability to follow the vet's instructions.

That said, don't be afraid to ask your vet questions or to ask him to do more research. Some long-time Pug owners know more about Pugs than do many vets. After all, Pug owners read about Pugs in books, magazines, and online. New information is being published, new research is being done, and questions are asked and answered. So listen to your vet, but at the same time, share your information with him, too.

A healthy Pug is always ready to play.

Vaccinations

Vaccinations work by giving your dog an inactive form of the disease so the dog can develop *antibodies* without the threat of actually getting sick. Most vaccines stimulate the body to produce antibodies for a period of time. Booster shots are then given to extend the protection.

A Pug from a breeder, shelter, or rescue group should have been started on a vaccination schedule. When you pick up your Pug, be sure you get a copy of those shots so your vet will know what to give your Pug.

Pug Speak
Antibodies are disease-fighting cells that help protect your dog from contracting the disease.

Rabies

Rabies is a virus and, when contracted, is always fatal. Your Pug can come in contact with rabies if he finds an infected wild animal such as a squirrel, bat, skunk, or fox. Once the virus is in the body,

Watch Out!
Never allow your Pug to play with a wild animal, especially one that doesn't run away from the dog or is otherwise acting strangely.

it affects the brain, causing changes in behavior (wild animals that are normally nocturnal will be active during the day) drooling, staggering, and seizures.

Distemper

Distemper is also a virus. Prior to the advent of distemper vaccinations, entire dog kennels would be wiped out within a period of days, with the virus moving from dog to dog to dog, killing them all. Distemper can be airborne and is picked up when one dog smells an infected dog's feces and inhales the virus. Dogs suffering from distemper will have a pronounced discharge from their eyes and nose.

Parvovirus

Parvovirus (often called parvo) is a very contagious, very dangerous virus that is most prevalent in younger and older dogs. Although veterinary care is saving more dogs infected with parvo, it is still one of the most dangerous viruses dogs can catch, partly because it hits hard and fast, but also because it mutates quickly. Vaccinations have to change, too, or they become ineffective. Parvo affects the intestinal tract, causing horrible diarrhea as well as vomiting. It is passed through contact with an infected dog's feces and can be tracked from one dog to another on a person's shoes.

Infectious Canine Hepatitis

This form of hepatitis is a virus that comes on very quickly; an infected dog can die within hours of the onset of the disease. It starts with a sore throat, and the dog will not eat or drink. The virus quickly moves to the liver and spreads to other organs. It is passed through direct contact with urine or nasal discharge.

Coronavirus

Coronavirus is a virus and, like parvo, is particularly severe in puppies. The diarrhea can lead to dehydration, but immediate veterinary care can save most puppies who catch it. Coronavirus is passed through contact with an infected dog's feces.

Leptospirosis

Leptospirosis is a bacterial infection that affects the kidneys. Symptoms include a fever, vomiting, and diarrhea, which can lead to dehydration. Antibiotics and supportive care can save some dogs, but many die because of the tremendous damage the bacteria cause. This bacteria is usually picked up in water that's been polluted with urine.

Kennel Cough

Several diseases fall under the kennel cough umbrella. Tracheobronchitis, adenovirus, and parainfluenza are three of the most common, but there are others. All are respiratory infections that are passed from dog to dog, usually by contact or by inhaling air with droplets of coughed matter. Most healthy dogs can recover from kennel cough with supportive care, but the very young and very old dogs are always at risk of secondary infections.

 Bet You Didn't Know
Kennel cough got its name because in a kennel situation, if one dog came down with it and began to cough, it would quickly spread throughout the kennel.

Other Dangerous Diseases

The list of diseases and their vaccinations is constantly changing. When Lyme disease became a problem a decade ago, there was no vaccine available, but there is one today, although not all veterinarians recommend it. West Nile vaccines have been introduced as well, although they are not yet recommended for dogs. Who knows whether they will be in the future. A vaccination is even being tested for rattlesnake venom.

Keep in touch with your veterinarian regarding threatening diseases and vaccinations. He will be up to date on what's available and can let you know whether anything's a problem in your area.

Potential Problems

Modern vaccinations have saved thousands of dogs' lives, but there are still potential problems with vaccines. These are serious medicine and should not be administered cavalierly.

Minor reactions to vaccinations can be as simple as a sterile abscess at the injection site. This appears as a hard lump several days after the injection. This will go away without treatment.

Pug Speak

Anaphylactic shock is a potentially fatal reaction to something the body regards as foreign matter. With vaccinations, this is the material injected into the dog's body.

Some dogs will have serious allergic reactions to one or more vaccinations. The reaction might be as mild as appearing lethargic for a day or two, or as severe as *anaphylactic shock*. Other dogs might develop problems later, including thyroid dysfunction or lameness.

In researching this book, I talked to more than 150 Pug owners and asked about their Pugs' reactions to vaccinations:

- 35 percent of the Pugs had no reaction at all to their vaccinations.

- 15 percent had a mild reaction that included soreness the day after or a sterile abscess.

🏠 35 percent had a moderate reaction that needed veterinary assistance, including medication.

🏠 10 percent had a serious reaction with life-saving veterinary assistance needed.

🏠 5 percent of the dogs died due to a reaction to a vaccination.

Because of the potential for a reaction, always remain at your vet's office for at least a half-hour after your Pug has received his shots just to be sure there's no problem. If your Pug has had a reaction before, your veterinarian might change his vaccination schedule, change what vaccines are given, and suggest medication prior to giving the vaccinations. Don't assume that because your Pug has never had a reaction he never will. Some dogs have a reaction after receiving several vaccines over time, while others have increasingly worse reactions after subsequent shots. Vaccination reactions are tough to predict and often seem to make no logical sense. They just happen.

Too Many Vaccines?

Many canine health professionals, veterinarians, breeders, and dog owners are questioning the time-honored practice of yearly booster vaccinations. Many are concerned that too many vaccines might overwhelm the dog's immune system, causing innumerable health problems later in life.

Some experts are also concerned about the vast numbers of vaccines being given. Modern medicine has given us vaccines to prevent many diseases that used to kill dogs, but in return, many dogs are suffering from immune system disorders and many more seem to be dying of cancer at younger ages.

 Watch Out!
Just because problems have been linked to vaccinations doesn't mean your dog should remain unvaccinated. These diseases have killed thousands of dogs prior to the introduction of the vaccines.

These problems have not yet been linked directly to vaccinations, but enough people are concerned that questions are being asked.

Many canine health professionals are recommending that vaccinations continue, but say the schedule can be restructured. For example, most puppies are given two to three vaccinations for distemper, hepatitis, leptospirosis, parvo and parainfluenza, and lepto. This five-in-one shot often makes puppies lethargic, grumpy, and sometimes even sick. However, it can be broken down so the distemper, hepatitis, and leptospirosis are given as one vaccination with parvo following in 2 weeks. Parainfluenza can then be given 2 weeks after that. The puppy's immune system would not be stressed as badly and also has time to recuperate between shots.

However, experts are quick to state that even this vaccination schedule can be a problem. Puppy shots are given when the immunities the puppy has from his mom are wearing off. If the vaccination schedule is spread out, the chances of the puppy getting sick are increased. There seems to be no easy answer.

Vaccinations for adult dogs are under just as much scrutiny. Booster shots have been given annually for many years, but many canine health professionals are now recommending stretching that to every 18 to 24 months. But not all agree.

Pug Smarts

The American Animal Hospital Association (AAHA) recently changed their recommendations concerning vaccinations and vaccination schedules. Learn more at www. aahanet.org.

This is an issue you must research yourself, find out as much as you can, then talk to your veterinarian. Find out what he knows and what his thoughts are. He will also know if any of these diseases are presently a danger in your community. This information can help the two of you make a more educated decision.

Vaccinate Only the Healthy

Only healthy puppies and adults should be vaccinated. Not only is the vaccine more effective if your Pug is healthy when he receives it, but the chances of your Pug having a reaction increase if his immune system is already stressed. If your Pug is taking any medications, ask your vet if those will affect how his immune system reacts to the vaccine. You might need to wait until the medications are completed before vaccinating your Pug.

When he is vaccinated, watch him closely. Report any reaction, even sleepiness, to your vet. A minor reaction today might signal the need for more observation for subsequent vaccinations.

Bet You Didn't Know

Give your Pug ¼ of a B complex vitamin twice daily beginning a week before he's scheduled to get a vaccination. Continue for a week after the shot. This will help his immune system cope.

Daily exercise is a must for a healthy, happy Pug.

The Importance of Spaying and Neutering

Most dogs should be *spayed* (if female) and *neutered* (if male). The only dogs who should be bred are those who have been proven to be the best representatives of the breed. The Pugs chosen to reproduce should have competed in conformation dog shows and earned their championship. Ideally, they should also have earned at least one obedience or agility title, and hopefully are also participating in some type of other activity, such as therapy dog work. They should be healthy, of good temperament, and of good genetic health, with healthy parents, grandparents, and siblings.

Pug Speak

When a veterinarian **spays** a female dog, he is removing the uterus and ovaries. When a male is **neutered**, or castrated, the testicles are removed.

Some Pug owners want to breed their beloved pet because they want another just like him (or her). But breeding a dog doesn't do that. Your Pug is what he is due to his genetic heritage, all his accumulated experiences, and you. If you bred your male, for example, his offspring would have a totally different set of genes than his because the offspring's genes would be a combination of your dog's and the female's. In addition, the offspring's experiences would be different. This would be a different dog.

Careful breeding is even more important today than it has ever been. Every day, thousands and thousands of dogs are destroyed in shelters all over the country—far too many of which are purebred dogs. Even the efforts of dedicated purebred rescue volunteers can't find homes for all these dogs. In addition, the list of genetic health threats facing purebred dogs, including Pugs, is growing.

Benefits of Spaying

When a female dog is spayed, her uterus and ovaries are removed through an incision in the abdomen. She'll need to be kept quiet for a few days so she can heal, but recuperation is usually very quick.

After she's spayed, your Pug will no longer come into season, ending that twice-a-year mess and hassle. Spayed females also have a decreased incidence of breast cancers later in life. Spaying also has a tendency to decrease female aggression. Spaying is best done prior to the first season, which often happens between 6 and 8 months of age.

Watch Out!
Pugs can have a tough time under anesthesia. I'll discuss which drugs to use (and which to avoid) in Chapter 12.

Bet You Didn't Know
Rumor has it spayed and neutered dogs will get fat, but this is a myth. Too much food and not enough exercise causes dogs to get fat.

Benefits of Neutering

When a male dog is neutered, the testicles are removed through a small incision just forward of the scrotum. This is also called castration. Healing is quick, usually with little reduction in activity.

Neutering males dogs eliminates the possibility of testicular cancer and reduces the likelihood of prostate problems. It also decreases many of the undesirable male behaviors such as leg-lifting, mounting, fighting, and roaming. Neutering to decrease male behavior is best done prior to the onset of adolescence, which can occur anywhere from 6 to 9 months of age.

The Difficulties of Breeding Pugs

Dogs have reproduced for thousands of years, with and without our help. But today, breeding dogs is different. Not only do dogs have some very serious genetic health threats, but today's dog breeds are different, too. The canine overpopulation problem also causes serious breeders to think twice before allowing a litter to be conceived.

Breeding Pugs is not an easy proposition, and as such, requires some serious thought. You must be able to research the ancestors of the male and female being considered for breeding. Were the ancestors of these two Pugs of correct physical conformation? Did any of their offspring have any problems, physically or temperamentally? Are the dogs being considered for breeding themselves correct (according to the breed standard), and are they healthy?

The breeding process can also be stressful. Sometimes the male will need help and often the female doesn't want to cooperate. You need to be able to assist them, and it's not always easy to do.

Once the litter is conceived, many female Pugs must give birth by caesarian section. The breed's big head does not make for easy whelping. Breeders must know when the female is having trouble so she can get veterinary assistance before she and the puppies are in trouble.

Most Pug mothers are good mothers, but there have been a few who want nothing to do with their babies. In these situations, the breeder must step in and care for the puppies. Then, the breeder must find knowledgeable, caring homes for the puppies and must be willing to take the puppies back should those homes not work out.

Pug owners who are really interested in breeding their beloved dogs need to make contact with a known, respected, and responsible Pug breeder; ask for help; then listen to the advice given.

The Least You Need to Know

- Your veterinarian is your partner in your Pug's good health.

- Vaccinations can help prevent many deadly diseases.

- Vaccinations can carry some risks, so talk to your veterinarian about shot schedules and the pros and cons of various vaccines.

- Most Pugs should be spayed or neutered. Only the very best should be bred and then only by knowledgeable breeders.

Chapter 12

Potential Pug Health Problems

In This Chapter

- 🏠 Making sense of Pug health problems
- 🏠 Supporting genetic testing and research
- 🏠 Don't panic—all Pugs are not unhealthy
- 🏠 Understanding senior Pug health threats

No one wants to think their treasured pet is sick or might possibly become sick. After all, most Pug owners chose this particular breed because it was sturdy (not fragile) and healthy. But Pugs, like many other breeds, can face some serious health threats. In this chapter, we'll take a look at these problems and just hope you never have to use this knowledge.

We'll also look at the problems older Pugs face. An old dog is a special kind of friend, one who knows you better than anyone else, and these friends need all the care and kindness we can give them.

Inherited Health Defects and Other Problems

Pugs are charming, appealing little clowns who make people laugh. They are sturdy, strong, and, for the most part, healthy. Often the only health threat many Pugs face is that of being too heavy. After all, obesity is just as dangerous for Pugs as it is for people.

Pug Speak

Genetic health problems are inherited. **Congenital health threats** are present at birth but might or might not be inherited.

Unfortunately, several health threats can reak havoc in your Pug's life—and yours. Some of these are *genetic health problems*, known to be inherited and passed from generation to generation. The origin of other *congenital health threats* is still being researched.

Although some Pug breeders are still burying their heads in the sand, ignoring the serious health threats faced by the breed, others are working hard to identify these dangers and find ways to eliminate them, if at all possible. Pug Dog Club of America Health Committee chairperson Christine Dresser, DVM, said the committee's goals are to identify and fund research on problems facing the breed. So far, the committee is working with the American Kennel Club's (AKC) Canine Health Foundation (CHF) to identify the DNA of normal, healthy, unaffected Pugs. Researchers will then, hopefully, be able to pinpoint DNA defects that could be markers for disease.

When health threats are found that require surgery, the breed's trouble with anesthesia adds another risk. Almost all Pug health experts recommend isoflurane as the anesthetic of choice and firmly state that acepromazine, ketamine, and xylazine should not be used (either alone or with other drugs), as too many Pugs have died while under the influence of these drugs. Keep the lines of communication open with your vet. Ask him what anesthetics he uses, and tell him what your concerns are and what research on the breed has found. If he's inflexible, perhaps it's time to find another vet.

The Eyes

Pugs have wonderful, expressive eyes, but unfortunately, those eyes have the potential for several serious problems:

- **Pigmentary keratitis (PK).** The first symptoms of this disease are normally dark spots on the white of the eye at the inside corner that can gradually spread over the surface of the eye. The brown pigment will obscure vision, even though the eye underneath it is still healthy. The cause of PK is still being debated, although most experts agree that inadequate tear production is probably one cause. Treatment usually consists of adding artificial tears to the eyes, treating any problems that might have caused the reduction in tears, and sometimes surgically removing the discolored outer layer of the cornea.

- **Generalized Progressive Retinal Atrophy (PRA).** This inherited disease causes middle-age dogs (5 to 7 years of age) to go blind. The disease causes a gradual degeneration of the retina, and currently there is no known cure. PRA is thought to be inherited, although the exact method of inheritance in Pugs is still being debated.

- **Keratoconjuctivitis sicca.** When looking at dogs with this disorder (also called dry eye), they do not appear to have normal wet eyes but instead have dull, dry-looking eyes. This disease can be caused by several different things, including a lack of tear production or a blockage in the tear ducts. Treatment will depend upon the cause of the lack of tears.

- **Corneal ulcers.** These are normally caused by an injury to the eye, such as a scratch, rather than an inherited cause. The breed's bulging eyes do make them more prone to injury than dogs with more protected eyes. Injuries to the eye should be treated immediately to be sure there will be no loss of sight.

Pugs have unique, globular eyes.

🏠 **Distichiasis.** This is a double row of eyelashes, usually on the lower eyelid. With two rows of lashes, several eye lashes are often pushed against the eye itself, causing irritation. Surgery is usually required to correct this.

🏠 **Entropian eyelids.** The eyelids roll in toward the eye, causing the eyelashes to irritate the eye. Surgery is normally needed to correct this.

The Nose and Mouth

The Pug's nose and mouth are deformed when compared to other breeds. With the shortened muzzle, the teeth are crammed together and usually crooked. The nose is flattened, and the airways are not always as open for breathing as they should be. These characteristics sometimes cause a number of different health challenges for the breed:

🐾 **Retained baby teeth.** At some point between 4 and 5 months of age, puppies begin to lose their baby teeth and the adult teeth come in. Sometimes an adult tooth will come in without the baby tooth falling out. A retained baby tooth can cause problems. Pushed against the adult tooth, it becomes a breeding ground for bacteria. In addition, a Pug's mouth is just too small for extra teeth. Any retained baby teeth should be pulled by your veterinarian.

🐾 **Crooked teeth.** Pugs have a smaller mouth yet have the same number of teeth other breeds of dogs have. As a result, a Pug's teeth are crowded, usually crooked, and often overlapping. Crooked and outward-pointing teeth, which irritate the inside of the Pug's mouth, should be pulled. Cleanliness of the teeth can help prevent other problems resulting from the overcrowding, such as bacterial infections of the gums.

🐾 **Stenotic nares.** The breed's extremely short muzzle can cause some breathing problems. In some Pugs, the nostrils are too small to allow enough air through, or the cartilage is too soft and the nostrils close while the dog is inhaling. The dog is constantly on the verge of suffocation and must breathe through his mouth. Surgery to open the nostrils and remove excess tissue around the nostrils can sometimes help.

🐾 **Elongated soft palate.** The soft palate is a structure of the mouth and nasal passages. If the soft palate is too long, it can make air passage to the lungs difficult. Although surgery can often correct it, it is a difficult, major surgery.

🐾 **Collapsed trachea.** The trachea is the breathing airway tube, and when under stress (such as overexertion or overheating), it might collapse and close, causing the dog to suffer breathing problems. Medications can ease this condition, but they must be at hand when the episode occurs. Surgery is usually not an option.

The Internal Organs

Luckily, Pugs do not have as many problems with their internal organs as do many other breeds. However, some of the problems Pugs do have can be serious:

- **Chronic obstructive pulmonary disease (COPD).** Pugs are prone to a variety of airway obstructions, all of which lead to stress on the respiratory system and heart, and to COPD. Treatment might be possible to open airway obstructions and to maximize heart and respiratory functions.

- **Liver shunt.** During fetal development, blood bypasses the liver because the mother dog's body cleanses the blood. Shortly after birth, this bypass should close, allowing the Pug puppy's liver to cleanse the blood. When the bypass does not close, the blood accumulates more and more toxins and wastes, and the dog gradually gets sick. This can often be corrected with surgery, although because the shunt must be closed gradually, it is a long surgery (4 to 6 hours).

The Nervous System

Luckily, Pugs do not have many problems with their nervous system, which includes the brain. Unfortunately, the problems Pugs do have are bad ones:

- **Pug Dog Encephalitis (PDE).** Encephalitis is an inflammation of the brain and the membranes covering the brain, the nerves, and spinal cord. The disease does, unfortunately, progress very rapidly, and there's no known treatment. Although there are other forms of encephalitis that other animals (including dogs) can get, this form of the disease has been found only in Pugs. The cause of the disease is still uncertain, although bacteria, fungi, and viruses have all been implicated. An inherited factor is also still being investigated. The first symptom of PDE is usually a seizure (or seizures), with abnormal behaviors (such as circling in one direction) beginning very soon after the first seizure. A magnetic resonance imaging (MRI) can provide a diagnosis.

🐾 **Idiopathic epilepsy.** Dogs can have seizures for many reasons, including head trauma, liver failure, or low blood sugar. PDE also causes seizures. When seizures occur and testing rules out other causes, the dog is said to have idiopathic epilepsy. Although there is no cure for epilepsy, it can be controlled in many dogs with medication. Epilepsy seems to appear in families of dogs within a breed (dogs who are closely related); however, the method of inheritance is still unknown.

The Skeletal System

The Pug is small and sturdy, but he can have some skeletal system (bones and the joints) problems:

🐾 **Hip dysplasia.** Most dog owners associate hip dysplasia with larger dog breeds, but Pugs can and do have a problem with hip dysplasia. In hip dysplasia, the head of the femur does not sit correctly in the hip socket. The joint then becomes very painful, causing the dog to limp or even refuse to move. Although surgery can often help those in great pain, it is not often recommended for small dogs simply because they are carrying less weight (than larger breed dogs), and hip dysplasia often does not seem to affect smaller dogs as severely.

Bet You Didn't Know

The Orthopedic Foundation for Animals (OFA) and the Pennsylvania Hip Improvement Program (PennHip) maintain lists of dogs who have been x-rayed for hip and elbow dysplasia. Breeders can research the lists and eliminate from their breeding program dogs with questionable elbows or hips.

🏠 **Elbow dysplasia.** Like hip dysplasia, elbow dysplasia is caused by a bone and joint deformity in elbow. The dog usually shows pain by limping on the affected front leg, and if the pain continues, the dog might stop using the leg entirely.

🏠 **Legg-Calve-Perthes disease.** With this disease, an insufficient blood flow to the femoral head causes the femoral head to degenerate. The first symptoms might be limping and progress to the point where the dog will no longer use the leg at all. Surgery is often needed to remove the necrotic bone.

🏠 **Luxated patella.** Also called slipped stifle, this is characterized by the dog hopping or skipping with one back leg elevated for a few steps. The kneecap on the back leg (called the patella) might be temporarily out of position, causing pinching and pain. The kneecap will move back on its own, and most dogs learn to stretch their leg to help it go back or cope by lifting that leg until the kneecap is repositioned, but surgery can correct severe cases.

🏠 **Hemivertibrae.** Pugs suffering from hemivertibrae have one or more incorrectly formed spinal vertebrae. If the vertebrae affected are in the neck, this can cause a curvature of the spine and even pressure on the spinal column, causing a loss of feeling and, in the worst cases, even paralysis.

The Skin

Pugs have a wonderful hair coat and normally, soft, unblemished skin, but they can still have skin problems:

🏠 **Allergies.** Although allergies affect the body as a whole, in Pugs, most allergies show up as skin allergies. The most common symptoms are chewing at the base of the tail, licking the paws, scratching, and chewing. Many Pugs have multiple allergies and might be allergic to foods, pollens, and a number of other things. Although there is no cure for allergies, testing can pinpoint specific problems, and treatment can lessen the impact.

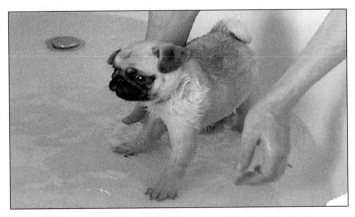

Pugs have a wonderful short coat, but can, unfortunately, have some skin issues.

🏠 **Demodex.** Demodex mange is caused by mites and usually appears as bald spots on the face. Untreated, this can be very serious, but young dogs treated early usually recover quickly.

🏠 **Pimples.** Pugs between 6 months and 2 years of age often develop pimples on their face. These pimples are minor skin infections, just like pimples on humans. Dogs prone to pimples should be fed on disposable paper plates or metal bowls, as plastic and ceramic bowls often harbor bacteria. Don't squeeze the pimples; just keep the Pug's face clean and let them run their course.

Senior Pug Health Challenges

Old Pugs might be gray around the face and might have slowed down considerably, but they are still charming and can act the clown when they want to. There is no friend in this universe like an old dog. Your old dog knows you better than anyone else; he knows your moods, your likes, and your dislikes, and he loves you with his entire being even on your worst days. Old dogs are treasures.

Unfortunately, old Pugs do face some health challenges:

- **Cataracts.** Cataracts can be caused by many different things—some inherited, some not. Most old dogs do develop some type of cataract at some point during their life. Talk to a veterinary eye specialist, as some cataracts can be corrected with surgery.

- **Incontinence.** Many old dogs reach a point where they leak urine, sometimes while sleeping or when waking up from a sound sleep. Others might leak urine all the time. Doggy diapers work very well for some dogs, although a few dogs will tear off the diapers. In some instances, a veterinarian might be able to prescribe medication that could control the incontinence.

- **Arthritis.** Arthritis is very common in older dogs. It can be worse in a particular bone or joint that was damaged earlier in the dog's life, such as a broken bone or in a joint affected with hip or elbow dysplasia. Arthritis usually shows up as slowness getting up, stiffness, and joint soreness. Your veterinarian might be able to prescribe medications to control (or lessen) the inflammation and pain.

Old Pugs might also suffer from heart, liver, or kidney disease, as do old dogs of all breeds. Your vet might recommend that your older Pug come in for an examination at least once per year, but don't panic if he wants to see your Pug more often. Senior dogs' health threats can come on suddenly; if your vet wants to see your dog more often, take him in. Your vet might also recommend regular blood tests to check liver and kidney function.

An old Pug is a treasured friend.

With good veterinary care, and with your loving supervision and care, a healthy Pug should live to 14 years of age with relatively little discomfort.

Saying Good-Bye

Although it's very difficult to discuss the passing of our treasured pets, it should be mentioned here. Very few dogs die in their sleep or pass away peacefully without pain or discomfort. A natural death is not always easy. Luckily, we do have the option of helping our pets along when the time is right. Deciding when the time is right can be tough, though. I have been lucky; my pets have been able to let me know when they were ready, either by refusing to eat or refusing to move, or by telling me in their own way.

You can take your Pug to the veterinarian's office, or your vet might come to your house to perform euthanasia. Usually the vet will give your dog a tranquilizer first so he is calm, then will follow

that with an overdose of a barbiturate. The dog will go to sleep, and his heart will stop. This process is incredibly difficult, but you can take comfort in knowing that you have done everything possible to keep your old dog happy, comfortable, and secure for his lifetime, including the end of his life.

The Least You Need to Know

- Pugs are, for the most part, healthy, sturdy small dogs.

- The breed's eyes are vulnerable to injury and are prone to several serious disorders.

- Some of the health threats faced by the breed are still being studied and might or might not be inherited.

- Old Pugs are a treasure. Work with your vet to maintain your old friend's health.

Chapter 13

Emergency First Aid

In This Chapter

- 🏠 Getting help when your Pug needs it
- 🏠 Assembling an emergency first-aid kit
- 🏠 Keeping your Pug safe and calm
- 🏠 Emergency first-aid guidance

Accidents and emergencies do happen, unfortunately, and often at the most unexpected times. All you can do is try to be as safe as possible with your Pug to prevent accidents, then be prepared to deal with whatever happens. Not only will you be able to deal with emergencies better when you're prepared, but you'll also have some peace of mind knowing that you've done the best you can do for your Pug.

Knowing Where to Get Help

When you initially talked to your veterinarian (see Chapter 4) you probably talked about *emergencies*. Not all veterinarians will open

Pug Speak

An **emergency** is a potentially life-threatening injury or illness or a health threat that cannot wait until the next business day.

Pug Smarts

Don't wait until you face an emergency to find out your vet's policies. Ask ahead of time so you know what to do and who to call.

after hours to see emergency cases, so you need to know if your vet does. If he does, ask a few questions:

- 🏠 How do you get in touch with him after hours?

- 🏠 Where does he do business after hours? Would you meet him at his clinic or at the local emergency clinic? Or does he come to your house?

- 🏠 What are his payment policies regarding emergencies?

If your veterinarian is not available for emergencies, where (or whom) does he suggest you call? Then call this veterinarian or the emergency animal clinic so you know how they do business.

- 🏠 Where is the clinic located? Be sure you know exactly where it is and can find it even when you're upset.

- 🏠 What are the payment policies? Most emergency clinics require payment in full upon services. If this is their policy, do you have a savings account or credit card set aside for emergencies? If you have pet health insurance, be sure it covers emergencies and the emergency clinic accepts it.

- 🏠 What happens after you bring in your dog? Will the clinic allow you to be present during treatment? Do they have the facilities to keep your Pug overnight? Just knowing what the standard procedures are will reassure you if you need to bring your dog in one day.

🏠 If your dog must remain overnight at the emergency clinic, what happens during business hours? Do you have to transfer your dog to your vet's clinic, or will they do that?

🏠 Will the clinic forward your dog's records to your vet? Or should your vet call the clinic? Or will you need to hand-carry the records to your vet?

Be sure you have your veterinarian's business card and the emergency animal clinic's card in several prominent locations. Have one in your first-aid kit, one in your wallet, one in the glove compartment of your car, and one on the refrigerator. When an emergency happens, it's easy to get upset and flustered, so make things as easy for yourself (and other family members) as possible.

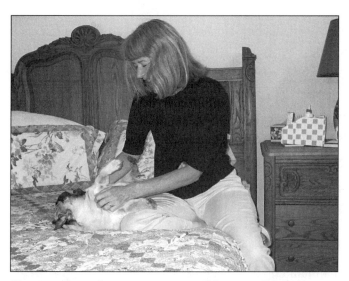

Knowing what to do in an emergency will keep your Pug happy, healthy, and safe.

Preparing an Emergency First-Aid Kit

My first-aid kit is famous—well, at least with my family and friends. When my husband and I were first married, we were evacuated from our house due to a threatening wildfire. I grabbed our pets and a few important papers, threw them in the car, and took off while he went to join the firefighters. It was 36 hours before I could get back to our house, and I had nothing in the car to help me—nothing! I swore that would never happen again.

Since then, I have carried a stocked first-aid kit in my vehicle, as well as emergency supplies such as water and a blanket. I also have extra leashes and collars and emergency rations. Although some people laugh at my efforts, they're always willing to use my supplies when the need arises!

I use a large fishing tackle box to hold all my supplies. On the outside I have written in large red letters "First-Aid Kit." I want it to be easily seen so if I send someone to my van who doesn't know what the kit looks like, he or she will be able to easily spot it.

Some supplies I keep in my kit and suggest you keep in yours include the following:

- Round-ended scissors and pointy scissors
- Heavy-duty trauma shears or scissors
- Large and small tweezers
- Disposable razors
- Small nail clippers (Pug size)
- Thermometer (rectal)
- Safety pins
- Mirror
- Pen, pencil, and paper for notes and directions

- Tape of various sizes, widths, and types

- Butterfly adhesive bandages

- Gauze pads of different sizes, including eye pads

- Elastic wrap bandages

- Instant cold compresses

- Antiseptic and antibacterial cleansing wipes

- Sterile saline eyewash

- A small bottle of first-aid wash for wounds

- A tube of antibiotic ointment

- Antihistamines

- Kaopectate tablets or liquid

- An extra leash and collar

I also keep a gallon jug of water, a dog bowl, and an old blanket in my van. You'll also need to keep on hand any medications your Pug needs. If he's had some problems with airway obstructions and you have emergency medications for him, keep those medications always available.

You'll need to check these supplies often so you can replace supplies that have been used and those that have expired. Most medications have an expiration date; don't use them after that date.

If you don't know how to use these supplies, consider enrolling in a Red Cross first-aid course. They offer informative courses for both human and canine first-aid. If the Red Cross doesn't have courses available in your area, ask a local veterinarian if he or she

Pug Smarts

To find out if or where your local Red Cross offers canine first-aid courses, call your local branch.

would be interested in teaching a class for a dog club or group for a modest fee.

Restraining Your Pug

Hurt dogs panic. They thrash, fight restraint, and bite, claw, and scratch anyone within reach. Many dog owners are unpleasantly surprised when their treasured pet bites them during an emergency. An injured dog isn't thinking clearly; all he knows is that he hurts and he doesn't know why. You need to know how to restrain your Pug so you don't get hurt, too, and so he doesn't hurt himself even more by struggling.

Dogs with a long nose can be muzzled to prevent biting, but we can't do that with Pugs. However, if you have help, you can still restrain him. Have one person restrain the Pug's head while another performs emergency first aid. With the Pug on a table or on a lap, have one person hold the Pug's head with a hand on either side of the head. The Pug's mouth will not be closed, so be careful to keep the mouth away from the person performing the first aid.

Because they're small, Pugs are easier to restrain than much larger dogs. But Pugs are strong little dogs and can wiggle and thrash with surprising strength. You don't want to restrain him by fighting him; that's going to get you both hurt. Instead, borrow a technique cat owners use called "bundling." The cat is snuggly wrapped in a blanket (with all four feet inside) with just the head showing. This not only keeps those well-armed paws out of action but also calms the cat. This technique works for Pugs, too. If you need to transport an injured Pug after first aid has been performed, wrap the Pug in a blanket (or big towel) snuggly enough to keep his feet inside but not tightly enough to restrict his breathing. Be sure he can breathe easily, and monitor him on the drive to the vet's office.

Watch Out!

Don't wrap up, or bundle, your Pug if he's overheated or potentially has a broken bone.

Canine CPR

Cardiopulmonary resuscitation (CPR) is a vital first-aid skill, but it takes some special care to perform it on Pugs. When you breathe for most dogs, you'll breathe into his nose with no problem. For Pugs, with their convoluted nasal passages, this can be difficult. It's always worth the effort, though, because without CPR, the dog might die.

When you come upon a Pug lying still, make a quick evaluation before doing anything else. Take the following steps, in this order:

1. Lift the dog carefully, moving him as little as possible (in case of other injuries) to a table, bench, or chair. Lay him on his side.

2. Check if he has a heartbeat by placing two fingers under either armpit.

3. Check whether he's breathing. Watch for his chest to move, or wet a fingertip and place it in front of his nose. You'll be able to feel his breath on your wet fingertip.

4. If he's not breathing, clear his mouth of any obstructions.

5. Pull his tongue out the side of his mouth so it doesn't block the airway.

6. Close his mouth over his tongue, and pull his lips around his teeth to help make his mouth airtight. Cup your hand around his lips and muzzle to hold them still and airtight.

7. Inhale a breath, then gently but firmly exhale into the Pug's nose. Watch his chest rise after you blow. (This might be harder than you expect due to the convoluted airways.) Don't exhale your entire breath. Remember,

Watch Out!

Don't practice CPR on a dog who isn't in a life-threatening situation. You could hurt him. Practice on a stuffed toy instead.

your lung capacity is much more than a Pug's. Just exhale a small breath, just enough to cause the chest to expand.

8. Repeat every 5 seconds if you can do so without hyperventilating yourself.

Watch Out! _____

When doing CPR on a Pug, you must compress his chest enough to move blood yet not hard enough to break his ribs. Be firm yet gentle.

9. After 10 breaths, stop and do chest compressions. With the Pug on his side, and using four fingers, compress his chest five times. Then go back to giving him air for 10 breaths, follow with then 5 compressions, then repeat.

Once you begin performing CPR, continue until the dog begins breathing on his own, until you can get the dog to the vet or emergency clinic, or until it's obvious your efforts are in vain. But don't stop too soon; many dogs have been saved by canine CPR.

Emergency First-Aid Guidelines

It can be very difficult to think clearly and logically in an emergency, especially when your dog is the one in danger. But every second and every move you make could mean the difference between saving your dog or losing him.

The emergency guidelines listed here aren't given to replace veterinary care. They are here to aid you in caring for your Pug until you can get him appropriate emergency veterinary care.

Bleeding

Bleeding occurs after just about any injury. How it should be treated depends upon the type of bleeding and its severity. If the skin isn't broken and there's some bleeding under the skin, treated it with an ice pack or a small bag of frozen vegetables makes a great ice pack. Place an ice pack wrapped in a hand towel or a T-shirt on the skin for 15 minutes, take it off for 15 minutes, and repeat until you get veterinary help.

Bleeding from small scrapes, scratches, and cuts is usually not a danger. Wipe it off, apply pressure with a gauze pad, and when the bleeding stops, wash it off with soap and water or an antibacterial wipe.

Continual oozing bleeding can be serious, as is spurting arterial bleeding. Put pressure on the wound, using layers of gauze pads and pressure from your hand, and get your dog to a vet immediately.

Watch Out!
Pugs are small dogs, and blood loss can quickly lead to shock and cardiac arrest.

Internal bleeding is very dangerous and less obvious. If your Pug has had a rough accident, especially if he's been kicked or dropped, watch him carefully. If he stops moving, cries, or acts restless, get him to the vet's office right away. Other symptoms of internal bleeding include pale gums, a distended abdomen, bloody diarrhea, bloody vomit, blood in the saliva, or coughing up blood.

Eye Injuries

Pugs are, unfortunately, prone to eye injuries. Although their large, protruding eyes are very much a part of the breed's appeal, their vulnerability causes problems. If something gets in the eye, such as a piece of grass, simply flushing the eye with a sterile saline eyewash is fine. However, if the eye has been scraped or punctured, or if the eye has come out of the socket, you'll need to get your dog immediate veterinary care to save his sight.

The most important thing to do is prevent your Pug from paw-
ing or scratching at his injured eye. He'll want to do this, but his
actions will only make the injury worse. This is a good time to bundle your Pug; wrap him securely and be sure all four feet are inside
the blanket.

Keep his eye moist, and if you have eye pads in your first-aid kit,
cover the eye. Don't use any first-aid products on the eye except
sterile saline eye wash unless you get directions from your vet via
the telephone.

Breathing Difficulties

With their convoluted and sometimes overly small nasal passages,
Pugs can and do have breathing problems. Preventing problems is
always best, of course. Pugs should not be exercised heavily in hot or
hot and humid weather, and they should be monitored during any
activities for heavy panting or gasping.

If your Pug has already been diagnosed with breathing difficulties and your veterinarian has prescribed medication, be sure you
have it with you whenever you and your Pug are out and about.
Sometimes Pug owners find that having the medication at home, in
the car, and in a small pack that goes with the dog's leash works well.

If your Pug has breathing difficulties and you don't have medication to control it, get to a vet right away. Untreated breathing problems could lead to heart problems, too, as well as shock.

Shock

A dog (just like a person) will go into shock after a traumatic injury
or during a serious, sudden illness. Shock is life-threatening, and
when combined with what caused the shock in the first place, your
Pug could be in serious danger of dying. Symptoms of shock include
pale gums, a rise in heart rate (often irregular), panting, gasping or
rapid breathing, dilated pupils with a staring look, and no response
to movement.

You cannot treat your Pug for shock, other than keeping him still and warm. You do need to get him emergency care immediately. When your dog is in shock, seconds count.

Heatstroke

An overheated Pug will pant heavily and gasp for air. He might pace back and forth, or he might throw himself on the floor. His body temperature will rise rapidly, and he might go into shock.

You need to cool your Pug immediately, even before you call your vet's emergency line. Put him in cool water or pack him in ice. Drive him to the vet's office while he's still in the cool water or ice.

Watch Out!

Never leave your dog alone in the car, even with the windows cracked. The air inside heats up very rapidly, even on cool days, and your dog could die of heatstroke before you return.

Poisons

Symptoms of poisoning can vary depending on the poison. Some of the more common symptoms include extreme salivation (drooling or frothing from the mouth), vomiting, diarrhea, and muscle tremors. The Pug's eyes might dilate, or he might suffer seizures.

Here are some of the more common household substances that are harmful to your dog and what you should do if your Pug gets into them:

- **Antifreeze.** Induce vomiting, and get your Pug to the vet right away.

- **Bleach.** Call your vet right away. He might want you to induce vomiting, or he might recommend you bring your Pug into his office immediately.

Bet You Didn't Know

You can make your Pug vomit by feeding him several teaspoons of hydrogen peroxide.

- 🐾 **Chocolate.** Make your Pug vomit, and call your vet.

- 🐾 **Gasoline.** Give your Pug some vegetable oil to block absorption, and get him to your vet's office right away.

- 🐾 **Ibuprofen.** Make him vomit, and take him to your vet's office right away.

- 🐾 **Insecticides.** Call your vet immediately, but do not induce vomiting unless your vet recommends it. If there was skin contact, wash him thoroughly right away.

- 🐾 **Rat, mouse, roach, or snail poisons.** Induce vomiting immediately, and get him to your vet's office.

Bet You Didn't Know

The National Poison Control Center 24-hour poison hotline is 1-900-680-0000. You don't need your credit card for this call; your phone bill will be charged.

In *every* situation where you even suspect your Pug might be poisoned, call your veterinarian. Bring whatever your Pug got into with you to the veterinarian's office, and be sure you have the box, bottle, or wrapper so your vet can read the ingredients and warnings or can call the manufacturer. The more information you can give your vet, the better.

Burns

There are several different types of burns. A chemical burn is caused by exposure to a corrosive substance, such as bleach, gasoline, drain cleaner, or road salt. Thermal burns are caused by heat, and electrical burns can occur when a dog chews through an electrical cord.

If you suspect your Pug has been burned, follow these directions:

1. If the burn is a chemical burn, rinse your Pug thoroughly. Treat it as a potential poisoning.

2. Put an ice pack on the burn.

3. If the burn is not severe and the skin is simply red, keep it clean and watch it to be sure it doesn't get infected.

4. If the burn is blistered, bleeding, and oozing, or has damaged any layers of skin, take your Pug to your vet's office right away.

Insect Bites and Stings

Some Pugs think chasing bees and wasps is great fun; unfortunately, those Pugs also get stung! If you suspect your Pug has been stung or bitten by an insect, try to find the stung spot on your Pug's body. If there is a stinger, scrape it out. Don't grab it and pull it out; that will only squeeze more venom into your dog. Scrape it out with a fingernail.

If you need to, shave some of the dog's hair so you can see the wound better. Wash it and watch it for any allergic reaction, including:

🐾 Swelling at the site and in the tissues around it

🐾 Redness or extreme whiteness

🐾 Fever

🐾 Muscle ache, joint pain, and lameness

🐾 Vomiting and/or diarrhea

🐾 Difficulty breathing

If your dog shows any of these allergic reactions, call your vet right away. He might recommend you give your Pug a Benadryl antihistamine immediately to combat some of the reaction. He'll also want to see your Pug right away.

Animal Bites

If your Pug has been bitten by another small dog during playtime and the bite is a simple puncture, don't be too worried. Wash it off, treat it with an antibiotic ointment, and watch it. If it looks red and inflamed, call your vet. Check with the owner of the other dog to be sure the dog is well vaccinated, especially for rabies.

If your Pug is attacked by a much larger dog, or an unknown dog, call your vet immediately, as this could pose a serious health threat. If you can, try to find the dog's owner to be sure the dog's vaccinations are up to date. Some bites might need special treatment, including but not limited to drains, sutures, and antibiotics.

Watch Out!

Wild animals carrying the rabies virus are not that uncommon. Skunks, raccoons, bats, and foxes have all been known to carry the disease. The best prevention is to be sure your Pug is vaccinated.

If your Pug is bitten by a cat or a wild animal, take him to the vet's office right away. Cat bites must be cleaned thoroughly, as they have a tendency to get infected. Bites from wild animals must also be treated, as there is a very real danger of rabies.

Snake Bites

If your Pug is bitten by a snake known to be nonvenomous, wash the wound with hydrogen peroxide or chlorhexidrine, and watch it to be sure the wound doesn't get infected.

If your Pug is bitten by a venomous snake, don't panic. As you grab your dog, take a good long look at the snake so you can describe it to your vet. What color is it? What color pattern? What was the shape of the head?

If a snake has injected your Pug with venom during the bite, the tissues around the bite will begin to swell. If your dog was bitten on the face, he'll need veterinary care right away, as he could be in danger of suffocating. Call ahead so your vet can begin making arrangements for antivenom.

Natural (and Other) Disasters

The fires that have devastated southern California in years past caught many people unprepared. Often, people were given just minutes to evacuate their homes and left with only the clothes on their backs—literally. But natural and other disasters can hit anywhere. Florida has hurricanes and sink holes, and the Midwest has tornadoes. Disasters can strike anywhere at any time. It's important to make preparations so you can take care of your Pug as well as your family.

I keep my first-aid kit in my van where it's easily accessible. It has both human and canine first-aid supplies. I also keep a gallon jug of water in the van, along with a couple blankets and extra leashes.

In the garage, within easy reach of the side door (so it can be reached even if the garage is damaged) I keep an emergency kit put together for fire evacuations or earthquakes. It has human and canine supplies, too. The canine supplies include canned dog food (which will keep for several years), a can opener, water, a smaller first-aid kit, and a variety of other emergency supplies.

A few of my neighbors think I'm either a little neurotic or overly concerned, but my husband and I have been evacuated from our home twice for wildfires and have survived several earthquakes. When you're ordered to evacuate, you don't have time to gather things; you grab what you can and leave. I would rather spend those few precious moments grabbing the dogs and cats and my emergency kit rather than putting the kit together in haste.

Think of the emergencies you might face in your region. If you live in a cold climate, be sure you have blankets and chemical hand warmers in your kit. In a hot region, you'll want to pack extra water. It never hurts to be prepared.

The Least You Need to Know

🏠 Know where to get help in an emergency, both from your veterinarian and from your local emergency animal clinic.

🏠 Know how to restrain your Pug in an emergency so he doesn't hurt himself and doesn't bite you in fear.

🏠 Put together a first-aid kit, and keep it well stocked and up to date.

🏠 Prepare yourself for an emergency now so you don't panic when and if an emergency strikes.

Part 4

The Gentleman (and Lady!) Pug

Many toy breed owners, including the owners of Pugs, assume that dog training is for "other" dogs—dogs other than toys, or other than Pugs. Dog training, however, is for all dogs and, rumors aside, Pugs are dogs!

In Part 4, I'll show you how to be your dog's teacher so you can teach him household rules, basic obedience commands, and anything else you might want him to learn later. I'll also talk about problem behaviors, including why Pugs get into trouble and what you can do to prevent or solve those problems.

The last chapter will take a look at why Pugs do some of the things they do, including some of the canine mysteries that have puzzled dog owners for eons!

You Are Your Pug's Teacher

In This Chapter

- 🏠 Knowing how to train your Pug
- 🏠 Training techniques and tools
- 🏠 Being your Pug's leader
- 🏠 Helping your Pug succeed

Rescue group volunteers, animal control shelter workers, and humane society staff will tell you that thousands of dogs are given up by their owners each year because of problem behaviors. Perhaps the dog dashed out the front door and wouldn't come back when the owner called, or maybe the dog had one too many housetraining accidents. Unfortunately, many of these dogs given up for bad behavior will never be adopted; they will be destroyed at the local shelters.

This happens all too often to Pugs, too. Pug puppies are incredibly cute and very easy to spoil and far too many Pug puppy owners do spoil them. However, a spoiled puppy is adorable; an adult dog who carries those bad puppy habits into adulthood is a brat. Bad habits get old real quick.

But giving up on your Pug isn't the solution! If you train him to be a good dog, he will be.

Learning How to Teach Your Pug

Dog training really should be called "dog and owner training." It's not something you do *to* your Pug; instead, training is something you, your family, and your Pug will all do together. During training, you'll be learning new things just as your Pug is. You might have to change some of your ideas about dog ownership as well as some of your household routines.

My dogs enjoy their training sessions, and yours should, too. Too many dog owners think of dog training as military boot camp, and unfortunately, years ago, a lot of dog training was like that. Today, however, we've learned that training doesn't have to be rough to be effective. In fact, if dog owners and their dogs both enjoy the training, it will be much more effective.

Bet You Didn't Know

Good dog training rewards desired actions or behaviors and discourages or prevents unwanted actions.

Teaching your Pug doesn't have to be difficult. Keeping a few thoughts in mind will help make training your Pug something you both enjoy:

🏠 **Communication.** How do you tell your Pug what you want him to do? First, you'll use a word, such as *Sit*. (I'll go through the specifics in Chapter 15.) You'll then help him assume the position of sit, then reward him for doing it.

The first few times you do this, your Pug probably won't understand what's happening. But at some point, the lightbulb will go on over his head, "Ah ha! Mom says this, I do this, and I get praised and a treat!" Once your Pug's had that breakthrough in understanding, training is much easier.

Praise. To be an effective trainer, you must also pay attention to your dog and reward the good things he does. We have a tendency to pay attention to the bad things our dogs do, but there isn't a dog alive who learned what to do by being yelled at. To learn what he's supposed to do to be a good dog, your dog needs praise, petting, or other positive reinforcements. When he walks past the kitchen trash can and doesn't look at it, praise him, "Good boy! Good to leave it alone!"

Pug Smarts

Using a scolding tone of voice to interrupt bad behavior can be effective at stopping that behavior, but it doesn't teach your dog what to do to be a good dog.

Consistency. Pug owners who become good trainers are also very consistent. Once you establish some household rules and begin obedience training, you must be consistent. If you don't want your Pug on the furniture, you—and every other person in your household—must enforce that rule every single day.

Repetition. Some dog owners expect their dog to learn the commands after just a few training sessions. Some dogs can learn this fast, but most do not. Training requires repetition. You'll have to practice these commands during training sessions, in the house during your daily routine, and out on your walks.

Pug Smarts

Training requires repetition, but not all at once. Keep training sessions short and sweet, and quit while your dog is still willing to do more. Several short training sessions are better than one long one.

🏠 **Patience.** Good dog trainers must also be patient. Training takes time, and it takes time for puppies to grow up and become mentally mature. Just make training your Pug a part of your lifestyle for a while.

The benefits of training your Pug depend on your goals. Even if you never plan on showing your dog in conformation dog shows or obedience trials, the benefits far outweigh the alternatives:

🏠 A trained Pug is housetrained in his own home and trustworthy in other people's homes as well.

🏠 A trained Pug won't dash out open doors, gates, or car doors.

🏠 A trained Pug can do more than an untrained Pug. He can play off leash because he will come when he's called.

🏠 A trained Pug is not destructive and is respectful of personal belongings.

🏠 A trained Pug is not a pest or a nuisance and doesn't try to be the center of attention all the time.

🏠 A trained Pug is fun to spend time with because he understands social rules and acceptable behavior.

🏠 A trained Pug looks up to his owner as his leader.

🏠 A trained Pug and owner share a bond of mutual respect. Both understand each other's strengths and weaknesses.

Bet You Didn't Know

A dog and owner who train together form a wonderful bond. He'll become so attuned to you it's almost as if he can read your mind.

Training Tools for Your Pug

You'll use training tools to help train your Pug. A leash is a training tool, as is your voice. Food treats and even a squeaky toy can all be used as training tools. Let's take a look at a variety of training tools so you can decide what will work best for you and for your Pug.

Books, Videos, or Classes: Which One?

In this and the next chapter, I'll give you a good description of how to teach your Pug the basic commands. I'll also discuss a number of the more commonly seen behavior problems. Is this going to be enough? For many Pugs and their owners, yes, it will be. Pugs who are basically good dogs and owners who have been able to establish a good relationship with their dogs might need only basic obedience training.

Other Pugs (and their owners) might need more help. Group classes provide socialization opportunities and a lot of distractions. Some dogs need this stimulation, while others need to learn to ignore the disruptions. Group classes are particularly good for puppies who need socialization.

A group training class is great socialization and teaches your Pug to pay attention to you amid distractions.

Private training is quieter and enables the instructor to tailor the instruction individually for each dog and owner. Some owners need this special attention, especially many first-time dog owners or the owners of a dog with behavior problems.

Videos put words into pictures. For dog owners who are very visual, this can be a good source of additional information.

Find what's going to work best for you and your Pug. It might be a combination of things—a group class supplemented by a video or a book, or maybe a private lesson or two to get you over a rough spot. It's up to you!

Using Leashes and Collars

Collars and leashes are training tools, too, just as your voice is. Use collars and leashes a lot during the training process to teach your Pug to listen to your voice. Although you want your dog to understand that he should listen to you when you talk to him, he doesn't know that yet, and the leash and collar can show him that he should listen to you.

You know you need a leash and collar when you take your dog out for a walk, but you can use them in other situations, too:

- When your Pug acts up around the house, getting into the trash can or stealing the kids' toys, put the leash on his collar and keep him close to you.

- When the kids are playing and the Pug chases them, nipping at their legs, put the leash on him and prevent him from chasing.

- When the family is eating and the dog is trying to beg under the table, put his leash on him and make him lie down away from the table.

- When guests come to the house, put your Pug on a leash so he doesn't annoy your guests.

You can use the leash and collar in many ways; these are just a small sample. I'll give you more examples as we cover the basic obedience commands in Chapter 15 and as discuss problem behaviors in Chapter 16. Meanwhile, get used to using the leash and collar. Just remember to take it off your Pug when you can't supervise him; you don't want him to get it tangled up and choke himself.

Following are some of the training collars and leashes you might use:

🏠 **Buckle collar.** A buckle collar is nylon or leather, fastens with a buckle of some kind, and holds your Pug's identification tags. This is the only collar many Pug's will need. It is soft, gentle, and doesn't give much of a correction.

Watch Out! _____

Always take the leash and training collar off your dog when you leave him alone. He could get tangled and choke if the leash is left on him.

🏠 **Training collar** (often referred to as a slip chain collar or choke chain). This collar works with a snap and release motion. Think of a bouncing tennis ball—snap (up) and release (down). *Never* jerk this collar hard, and *never* hold it tight. Don't allow your dog to pull it tight, either, as it can choke him. When you use this collar to give a correction, always use your voice. "Acckk! No pull!" while you snap and release. Otherwise, your Pug might think the snap is simply a movement on your part without any meaning. This collar can be a very useful training tool when used correctly; it can also be dangerous when improperly used.

Pug Smarts _____

Head halters are very popular training tools right now. They're much like a horse halter and are very gentle. They should never be used on Pugs, though. Pugs don't have enough muzzle to use them effectively.

🐾 **Chest harnesses.** Many Pug owners prefer to use chest harnesses on their Pugs rather than collars. The assumption is that a chest harness will cause less damage to the dog than a collar around the neck will do. This assumption is not true, however. Pugs wearing a chest harness still pull on the leash and often pull harder than they do when wearing a collar. As they pull, they put pressure on their chest, shoulders, and back, and many end up with serious shoulder problems. A chest harness is fine as long as the Pug doesn't pull on the leash, but a harness won't stop the pulling.

🐾 **Leash.** A leash, either a regular-length or a long one, attaches to the collar or halter so you have a means of using the collar or halter to teach your Pug. A collar alone won't do much; you must be able to use it. That's where the leash comes in.

🐾 **Rigid leash.** A rigid leash is an excellent tool for owners of toy breed dogs to use. This isn't a leash you'll find at a pet supply store; you'll have to make it yourself. Buy an inexpensive, 4-foot-long lightweight cotton web or nylon leash at a pet supply store. At a craft or hardware store, buy a 3-foot-long wooden dowel about ½ inch thick. Lay the leash up against the dowel, with about 3 inches of the leash, including the snap, hanging off the bottom. The loop for your hand should hang loose at the top. Fasten the leash securely to the dowel along the entire length with screws or wood staples. If you want, you can wind duct tape along the length of the dowel for added security. This will give you a solid leash to help you teach your dog without having to bend to his height quite as often you might otherwise need to do.

Pug Smarts

To keep a motivator special, give it to your Pug only when you are working with him. Never give it to him "just because."

🐾 **Motivators and positive reinforcements.** These are things your Pug likes, including food treats, squeaky toys, furry toys, or even a tennis ball. They can be used to help your Pug do what you want (as a lure, for example) or as a reward for doing something right.

Use your training tools as much as possible. If you use them only during training sessions, your Pug will think they're for use only during training sessions and, therefore, the behavior he is learning during those sessions is also only for use then. Instead, use these training tools often during your daily routine.

Using Your Voice

I teach all my training class students that they should consider their voice their ultimate and most important training tool. Their eventual goal—and yours with your Pug—should be to teach the dog to listen to you when you talk to him. That means he should come when you call him and stop sniffing the trash can when you catch him with his nose in it. You want your Pug to understand that your words mean something and are not just noise.

To make it easier for your Pug to understand, you'll be copying some of the mother dog's verbalizations—or at least her tone of voice. When your Pug was still with his mom, he would interact with her and his littermates using verbal sounds as well as *body language*. If he wanted to play, his bark was higher in pitch. If a littermate or his mom responded to his play invitation, their barks were also higher in pitch.

Pug Speak _____

Dogs use **body language** as a means of communication. Facial expressions, coat markings, body postures, and movements all make up canine body language. How are coat markings body language? They emphasize the movement of the skin under them. Ever wondered why so many breeds have tan or black eyebrows or marking above the eyes? When that flash of color moves with the skin, it emphasizes the expression and makes it more noticeable. The same with lighter or darker colors on the muzzle. When a dog with a black muzzle snarls and bares those white teeth, it's much more noticeable.

When praising your Pug, say "Good boy!" in the tone of voice you used as a child to say "Ice cream!" This should be higher in tone from your normal speaking voice but not as high-pitched as a yelp that would mean you were hurt.

Bet You Didn't Know

Many women complain that their dog listens to their husband better than he does to them. Why? Men's voices are deeper and, therefore, carry more authority to the dog!

When your Pug was corrected by his mom, for example if he bit her with his needle-sharp baby teeth, she would growl at him. That deep growl meant, "You made a mistake! Don't do it again." We can use this sound, too. When your Pug makes a mistake, you can use a deep voice to make a sound such as "Acckk!"

There's no way we can sound like a dog—even with lots of practice! But try to use your voice in the same way your Pug's mom used hers: higher pitched for happy, very high pitched for hurt, and deeper for correction. By using tones much like she used, you can keep confusion during training to a minimum.

Pug Smarts

If you're normally soft spoken and are concerned about using your voice to control your Pug, don't worry. You're not going to scream and shout. Use your normal speaking volume, but vary the tones just as someone else would do who speaks louder. You're teaching your Pug to listen to you, and if you are naturally soft spoken, that's fine. Your Pug can hear you very well.

Teaching Your Pug

Every dog trainer has his or her own preferred method of training dogs. As long as the method is humane and effective, there's no right or wrong way. In this and the next few chapters, I'll be introducing you to the techniques I have been developing and using for the past 25 years in my dog training classes.

My training techniques are called "balanced training." I use a balance of *positive reinforcements* to reward the dog for doing something right and *interruptions* to stop behaviors we don't want to happen again. The primary emphasis is on the positive.

Pug Speak

A positive reinforcement is something the dog likes, such as food treats, a toy, petting, and verbal praise. An **interruption** stops a behavior as it is occurring.

Not only do I use these techniques in my classes, but also with my own dogs. Knowing I use exactly the same techniques when raising one of my puppies, my students can watch my dogs and see what's possible with the training if they persist and follow through with it. Not only that, my students (and you) can see that I have enough faith in what I am teaching you to use it with my own dogs.

If you're working with a dog trainer whose techniques are different from mine, that's fine. What is important is that you find a technique comfortable for you because you need to participate in this process and believe in it. If you're ambivalent about it, you won't be successful.

Bet You Didn't Know

Learning is an ongoing process. Every time you interact with your Pug, you teach him something and it might (or might not) be what you want him to know! Think about it—what are you teaching him right now? For example, if your Pug barks at another dog, what do you do? If you pet him and tell him, "It's okay, Sweetie, that dog won't hurt you," you're praising him for barking. Your petting and soft words are praise, so you're telling him it's okay to bark at other dogs. As you interact with your dog, try to find some other examples of communication that you might have messed up.

Emphasizing the Positive

What do you do when your Pug does something wrong? Say, for example, you find toilet paper spread all over the bathroom and down the hall? This is a common puppy trick. If you're like many dog owners, the first thing you do is yell, "What did you do? Oh, bad dog! Shame, shame, shame!"

But did this teach your dog anything? Probably not. Oh, he might think you're unpredictable or slightly unbalanced. He might think you dislike toilet paper. But I doubt very much he learned that he's not supposed to unroll and shred toilet paper.

Why not? First, because timing is critically important. If you caught him as he was pulling the toilet paper off the roll, you could then use your voice and scold him. But when you come upon the mess with the paper unrolled and your Pug already out of sight, it's too late. You have to catch him in the act.

In addition, you have to learn to prevent the problem from happening. Close the bathroom door or put up a baby gate so he can't get in the hall where the bathroom is.

Keep in mind, too, that dogs do not learn what to do by being corrected. An interruption can let the dog know when he's made a mistake, but it cannot tell the dog what to do instead. Positive reinforcements do let your dog know when he did something right.

For example, let's look at the toilet paper problem again, this time with a positive point of view:

- He's tearing up the toilet paper because it's fun. This makes the activity self-rewarding.

- Prevent him from getting at the toilet paper as much as realistically possible.

- When you catch him in the act, interrupt him so you stop the behavior as it's happening.

- When he comes into the bathroom with you and ignores the toilet paper, praise him and give him one of his own toys to play with.

You can approach much of your Pug's training in this manner. Let him know when's made a mistake, but show him the right way and praise him enthusiastically when he does it right.

> **Pug Smarts**
>
> *Always* praise your Pug when he does something right.

Keep training fun for both you and your Pug.

The Agony of Negative Attention

Because so many dog owners respond to everything bad their dogs do by yelling, many dogs learn that doing things wrong is a sure way to get their owners' attention. These dogs will put up with anything because it's still attention from their owner.

To change this scenario, the owner must focus on giving the dog attention for good behavior. This might be difficult in the beginning because we have a tendency to react to things we don't like. However, when the negative attention decreases and the good behavior is rewarded, the dog's focus will change.

Being Your Pug's Leader

I always stress leadership in my training classes. Puppies and young dogs naturally look to someone older for leadership, just as young human children do. The parents and other adults are (or should be) natural leaders. Without leadership, the young would not grow up to know social rules and how to survive.

Pug Smarts

To be a good leader for your Pug, think of being a good parent.

People who own larger-breed dogs, especially those that can be quite powerful and dominant, seem to realize that they must assert themselves to be their dog's leader. Unfortunately, many small dog owners don't seem to understand that it's just as important for their dogs.

Dogs are dogs are dogs, and size is immaterial. For good mental health, your Pug needs a leader, and it must be you. If you don't assume the leadership position, your Pug will suffer for it. I have had (and will have more in the future) dog owners call me with a whole list of their dogs' behavior problems—the dog urinates in the house, growls when the owner tries to do anything, sleeps at the head of the bed and growls when the owner moves, and a variety of other bad behaviors. The vast majority of these behaviors have developed because the dog is in charge, not the owner.

As the leader, you must make certain things happen:

🏠 Train your dog. Be fair and positive, but train him.

🏠 The leader is confident. If you are not yet confident about your role as leader, at least act like it!

🏠 You should always eat first, even if it's just a carrot. The leader of the pack always eats first and best.

🏠 Feed your Pug set meals at scheduled mealtimes. Do not free feed (leave food out all the time).

🏠 The leader always goes first. Make him wait for you to go through doorways first. Then give him permission to follow you.

🏠 Do not allow him to growl at you, ever!

Watch Out! ___

If your Pug growls at, snaps, or tries to bite you, call a professional trainer or behaviorist for help right away!

Be your Pug's leader. It's better for both of you.

Most people add a dog to their family because they want a companion. Most people envision a dog like Lassie or Rin Tin Tin—a canine best friend. Your Pug can be your best friend someday, but first you must be his leader. Later, when your leadership is undisputed and when your Pug is well behaved and well trained, he can become your best friend.

In the canine world, affection, leadership, and respect all go together. If you are not your dog's leader, you won't be respected and will be thought of as weak. Be strong and confident, and your dog will recognize you as his leader.

Setting Up Your Pug for Success

Training shouldn't be something horrible you or your dog dread doing. Instead, make it a part of your daily life and keep it upbeat and happy. You can make your training more successful by following a few guidelines:

🏠 Teach your Pug. He wasn't born knowing what the word *Sit* means. You have to teach him. Show him what to do, help him do it, and praise and reward him when he cooperates.

🏠 Do not repeat commands over and over again. That just teaches your Pug to ignore you. Plus, if you repeat it, which time counts? Which one should he respond to? Say a command once, then help him do it.

🏠 Be consistent. Once you establish some rules—such as not dashing out open doors—you must consistently enforce them.

🏠 Timing is critical to your training success. Praise your Pug *as* he is doing something right. Interrupt your Pug *as* he makes a mistake. Reactions that happen later are not effective.

 Watch Out!

Don't train your Pug when you're tired, frustrated, or angry. You don't want to take out those negative emotions out on your dog.

🏠 Involve the family. Everyone in the family should know how to train your Pug, and everyone should consistently enforce the training rules.

Finish every training session with a success. Stop when your Pug has successfully learned something or when he does something very well. You and he will both finish the session feeling good. If your Pug is having a hard time with a particular lesson, ask him to do something you know he can do and can do well. After he does it, stop the training session there. You can then still stop on high note.

No Excuses!

Don't make excuses for your Pug. Pugs might be small, but they do have a fully developed brain. They are bright, alert, intelligent dogs who can and have thrived on training.

When teaching Pug owners, I often hear the following excuses:

🏠 **"He's so small, he can't do that."** There's nothing in basic obedience that a Pug cannot do.

🏠 **"Pug's can't go to group training classes because they aren't like other dogs."** Pugs are unique, we know that, but they can still benefit from a group training class.

🏠 **"I don't take him for walks because he can't breathe well."** Pugs can have difficulty breathing, especially in hot, humid weather, but there's no reason why a healthy Pug can't go for daily walks. Just vary the length and speed of the walk according to the weather.

So no more excuses! Your Pug might be unique, but he's a dog! Let him be a well-trained one.

The Least You Need to Know

🏠 Training has benefits for you, your family, and your Pug. It's something you all participate in.

🏠 You can use a variety of training techniques and tools to teach your Pug.

🏠 Teach your Pug by helping him do something right and then praising him for it.

🏠 You must be your Pug's leader before you can be his best friend.

Chapter 15

The Eight Basic Obedience Commands

In This Chapter

- 🏠 The importance of basic obedience commands
- 🏠 Training the basic commands
- 🏠 Using the commands at home and out in public
- 🏠 Making the training successful

The eight basic obedience commands are: "Come," "Sit," "Release," "Lie down," "Stay," "Watch me," "Let's go," and "Heel." These commands should be a part of every Pug's vocabulary, not just because it's traditional to teach them, but because these commands are the foundation for everything else you'll do with your Pug. If you want to let him play off leash, he really can't until he comes to you reliably when you call him. Walking a dog isn't any fun if he's constantly pulling, plus it's bad for his neck, shoulders, and back. If you decide to have your Pug do therapy dog work or play in agility, the basic commands are necessary for that, too.

Starting With the Basics

Before we actually begin training, does your Pug know his name? When you say, "Sweetie!" for example, does he look at you? For a few days before you begin training, have some really good doggy treats and some special toys at hand, and every once in a while, simply say your dog's name in a very happy, upbeat tone of voice. After saying his name, toss him a treat or a toy, and praise him.

Your goal is to have your dog react in a happy manner when he hears his name, turn toward you, and wait for something else to happen.

Pug Smarts

You'll be using treats during your Pug's training, so cut back on his regular food just a little and watch his weight.

With the basic obedience commands, your Pug will learn that you can set some rules, ask him to do some things, and good things happen when he cooperates. Some dogs learn this very easily, while others have a harder time with it. In any case, be patient. Remember, you are *both* learning.

Teaching "Sit"

Teaching your Pug to *sit* is relatively easy. Teaching him to sit still is a little harder, but we'll take this in small steps and set him up to succeed.

Pug Speak

Sit means, "Lower your hips to the ground, keeping your front end up, and hold still."

Attach the regular leash (not the rigid leash) on your Pug and hold it in one hand, with a treat in the other hand. Show him the treat. When he reaches up to sniff the treat, move it back over his head toward his tail as you tell him, "Sweetie, sit." When his head comes up and back to follow the treat, his hips will go down. After he sits, praise him and give him the treat.

If he spins around to try to get the treat rather than sit, put away the treat in your pocket. Put one hand where his chest and neck meet. Tell him, "Sweetie, sit," and at the same time, push his chest up and back as the other hand slides down his back and tucks his hips down and under. Think of a teeter-totter—up and back at the chest, and down and under at the hips. When he's sitting, praise him. You want your Pug to understand that "Sit" means, "Put your hips on the ground, keeping your front end up, and be still."

Bet You Didn't Know
You can't tell your Pug what you want him to do and expect him to understand the words, so you must teach him what those words mean. You do this using your training tools, your voice, your hands to shape him and pet him, and treats.

When he does sit, praise him with a higher-than-normal tone of voice, "Good boy to sit!" When he begins to move from the sit position, use your growling tone of voice, "Acckk!" and put him back in the sit position.

The sit command is very useful, not just as the foundation command for more advanced commands, but also for use around the house:

🏠 Have him sit before you give him a treat or feed him. He can't sit, jump on you, and claw your legs at the same time!

Pug Smarts
When your Pug learns to sit on command, he also learns to control his own actions. Self-control is a hard—but important—lesson to learn.

🏠 Have your Pug sit to greet people, especially if he likes to scratch their legs. He should learn to sit still for petting.

🏠 Have him sit when you hook up his leash to take him outside. If he's sitting, he can't be spinning around in circles out of excitement.

🏠 When he wants you to play with him, have him sit first. Have him sit each time you go to throw his ball or toy.

Sit is a great control command and the foundation for all subsequent commands.

Teaching "Release"

Your Pug needs a beginning and an end to each command. The beginning is his name. When you say, "Sweetie," he knows you're talking to him and he should listen. The *release* is a command that means, "Okay, you're done now, you can move." With the release command, your Pug knows exactly when he's allowed to move from position or a previous command. It alleviates confusion; he knows when he's done.

Pug Speak
Release means, "Okay, you can move now. You're done."

With your Pug sitting, tell him, "Sweetie, release!" in a high-pitched tone of voice. Use the leash to gently move him from the sit.

Teaching "Lie Down"

Have your Pug sit and praise him. With a treat in one hand and another hand (the one with the leash) on your Pug's shoulder, tell him, "Sweetie, *lie down*," as you let him sniff the treat. Move the treat directly to the ground in front of his front paws. (Lead his nose down with the treat.) As he starts to move down, the hand on his shoulder can be assisting him in this downward movement. However, don't push! If you push, he might simply push back. Instead, just let the weight of your hand rest on his shoulders. When he's down, give him the treat and praise him.

When you're ready for him to move, give him the release command. Using the leash, encourage him to move. The release from the down should mean the same thing as it did in the sit, "You're done now. You can move."

Pug Speak

Lie down means, "Lie down on the floor or ground and hold still."

The lie down command is very useful, both in the house and in public. You'll use the lie down in conjunction with the stay command (which we'll learn next):

- Have your Pug lie down during meals so he isn't begging under the table. Place him where you can see him but away from the table.

- Have him lie down at your feet or on the sofa next to you while you're talking to guests. He can't be jumping all over them or knocking over their drinks if he's being still.

- Have him lie down and give him a toy to chew on when you would like to have some quiet time to read or watch television.

- Have him lie down while you're talking to a neighbor.

- Have him lie down while you get your mail out of the box and sort through it.

Teaching "Stay"

The *stay* command is used with the sit and lie down commands. You want your Pug to understand that "Stay" means "Remain in this particular position while I walk away, and remain here until I come back to you and release you." The sit and lie down commands by themselves teach your Pug to hold that position until you release him—but only while you're with him. With stay, you'll be able to walk away from him and know he's sitting still.

Have your Pug sit. With the leash in one hand, hold the other hand in front of his face as if you were building an invisible wall in front of his nose. Tell him, "Sweetie, stay!" and take a half-step away from him. If he moves, use your voice, "Acckk!" and put him back in position. Wait a few seconds and then step back to him. Have him hold still while you praise and pet him, then let him move with the release command.

Pug Speak

Stay means, "Hold this position until I come back to you and release you."

After practicing the stay with the sit for a few days, try it with the lie down. The training methods are the same except you'll have your Pug lie down. However, *you* tell your Pug which to do. If you ask him to sit-stay and he decides to lie down, correct him and help him back up in to a sit. He doesn't get to choose which exercise—you do.

Don't be in a hurry to move away from your Pug or have him hold the stay for long periods of time. It's very difficult for puppies and young dogs to hold still for any amount of time, and right now it's more important that your Pug succeeds in his training.

Use the stay around the house in conjunction with the sit and lie down:

🏠 When guests come over, have your Pug lie down by your feet or on the sofa by your side and tell him to stay. Then he can't be pestering your guests. He can visit with your guests when he's calm.

🏠 When you want him to stay away from the table while you're eating, have him lie down and tell him stay. You can give him a dog bed or a rug to lie on so he has a specific spot all his own.

🏠 Tell him to sit and stay while you're fixing his dinner so he doesn't jump all over you and or trip you.

🏠 Have him sit and stay at doorways, gates, and at the curb so you can teach him to wait for permission.

🏠 Tell him to sit and stay in the car so when you open the car door he doesn't jump out unexpectedly.

There are lots of uses for these commands. Just look at your house, your routine, and where you might be having some problems with your Pug's behavior. Where can the stay help?

Teaching "Come"

The *come* is a very important command; one that could potentially save your Pug's life some day. When I teach my dogs to come when called, I want them to understand that "Come" means, "Stop what you're doing and come back to me right now, with no hesitation, as fast as you can run." This instant response might save your dog from a dangerous situation—perhaps being attacked by aggressive dog, being hit by a car, or being bit by a snake in the grass. Situations come up every day that could cause your Pug harm; a good response to the come command could save his life.

With your Pug on his leash, hold the leash in one hand and have some treats in the other. Back away from your Pug as you call him, "Sweetie, come!" Be sure you back up a few steps so he gets a chance to chase you. If he doesn't come to you right away, use the leash to make sure he does. Pop a treat in his mouth, and praise him when he does come to you, "Good boy to come!"

Pug Speak

Come means, "Come directly to me, without hesitation or detours, as fast as you can

Also practice this with a long leash. Regular long leashes can be too heavy for a Pug, so try a lightweight nylon rope. Cut a 20-foot length of the rope and fasten it to your Pug's collar. Practice the come the same way you did on the leash. Keep the command very positive as you call him.

Come is an important—and potentially life-saving—command.

As your Pug learns the come exercise and responds well to it, add some games to the practice. Call him back and forth between two family members, and offer him a treat each time he comes. Be sure you keep it fun and exciting.

If your Pug hesitates about coming to you when he's off leash—especially if something is distracting him—there are some tricks you can use to make him come to you. First, don't chase him. That will only make him run farther and faster away from you. Instead, call his name in an exciting (not scolding) tone of voice and then run away from him. At that point, many dogs will turn and chase after you!

Some other tricks will bring your Pug in closer to you. You can lie down on the ground, hide your face, and call him. Or bend over and scratch at the ground as if you're looking at something very interesting. Ask your Pug, "What's that?" in an "Ice cream!" tone of voice. When he gets up to you, don't reach out and grab him saying, "Ah ha!" You'll never fool him again. Instead, continue to talk to him in an excited tone of voice as you gently take hold of his collar and praise him for coming to you.

Watch Out!

Never scold your Pug for anything to do with the come command. Timing is vitally important, and if he misunderstands a correction, he could learn that coming to you is bad.

For safety's sake, try to prevent come problems by limiting your Pug's time off leash, especially outside of your fenced in yard. If he's off leash and ignores your come command, he's just learned that he doesn't have to do it and there's not much you can do about it. However, if you let him play while dragging that long leash, then when he ignores you, can make him come to you when you call him simply by using the leash. Although allowing our Pugs to have the freedom to run and play is attractive, it shouldn't happen until the Pug is all grown up and very well trained.

Teaching "Watch Me"

Training your Pug can be very difficult if you can't get him to pay attention to you. Most dogs will focus on their owner at home, but when you're out in public, your Pug might want to pay attention to everything but you! You can help your Pug succeed by teaching him the *watch me* command.

Pug Speak _____

Watch me means, "Pay attention to me, and ignore distractions."

The goal of the watch me command is to teach your Pug to look at you, preferably your face and your eyes. Your Pug needs to ignore any distractions that might be occurring around him and focus on you. In the beginning, this focus might only last a few seconds, but later, as your Pug gets better at it and as his concentration gets better, he should be able to focus on you and ignore distractions for minutes at a time.

With his leash in one hand, have your Pug sit in front of you. Bend over or kneel down so your face is closer to him than it is when you are standing erect. With treats in the other hand, tell him, "Sweetie, watch me!" At the same time, let him sniff the treat and take it up to your chin. This movement and position is important. Let your Pug sniff the treat so he knows you have it. Take it up to your chin (slowly) so that as he watches the treat, his eyes follow your hand to your face. As he looks at the treat and then at your face, praise him, "Good boy to watch me!" then pop the treat in his mouth. If he gets distracted and looks away, take the treat back to his nose and get his attention back to you.

Pug Smarts _____

Be sure you use a treat your Pug really likes and save that treat just for training sessions. Keep it special!

When he's doing the watch me fairly well, stand up again and ask your Pug to watch you. If he doesn't, or if he looks away, give a verbal correction, "Acckk!" and repeat the command. As soon as he looks back at you, praise him.

As your Pug learns watch me, you can start making it more challenging. Tell your Pug, "Sweetie, watch me!" then back away from your Pug so he has to watch you while he's walking. When he can follow you for a few steps, back up in a zigzag pattern, making turns and corners. Back up quickly, then slowly. Add some challenges. Of course, when your Pug can do this, and has fun following you, you should praise him enthusiastically!

Teaching "Let's Go!"

Good on-leash skills are necessary for all dogs. When on leash, the dog should respect the leash without fighting it, pulling on it, or choking himself on it. The "Let's go!" command will help teach those skills.

With your Pug on the soft leash, hold the end of the leash in one hand, tell him, "Sweetie, *let's go!*" and simply back away from him. If he watches you, praise him. If he follows you, praise him even more. However, if he sniffs the ground, looks away from you, or tries to pull the other direction, use a verbal interruption, "Acckk! No pull!" (Or "No sniff," if that's appropriate.) After the interruption, if he looks back up to you, praise him.

Pug Speak

Let's go means, "Follow me on the leash, keeping it slack, with no pulling."

Back away from your Pug several times in several different directions. Each time he follows you and each time he looks up at you, praise him. Every time he pulls away, sniffs the ground, or ignores you, interrupt him. Your goal is to have your Pug keep the leash slack as he follows you, paying attention to your every move. And of course, when he does, praise him enthusiastically!

Teaching "Heel"

The "*Heel*" command means, "Walk by my left side with your neck and shoulder area next to my left leg, maintaining that position no matter what I do." With that definition, if you walk fast, jog, walk slow, or simply amble, your Pug should maintain his position. If you go for a walk through crowd and have to zigzag through people, your dog should still maintain that position.

Pug Speak

Heel means, "Walk by my left side, with your shoulder next to my left leg."

Teaching the heel, however, requires a great deal of concentration on your Pug's part. *Do not* start teaching the heel until your Pug has been doing the watch me for several weeks (not days—*weeks!*) and has been doing the let's go very well for at least 2 weeks with regular practice.

Place your Pug on the rigid leash (it will make this exercise much easier than the regular soft leash would). Hold the leash in your left hand and some treats in the right. Back away from your Pug as you tell him, "Sweetie, let's go!" As he follows you, let him catch up with you as you back slightly and turn so you're facing the direction he's walking and he ends up on your left side. Walk forward together as you show him a treat and tell him, "Sweetie, heel!" Stop after a few steps, have him sit, and praise him as you give him the treat.

Repeat this several times, keeping each walking session short, enthusiastic, and fun. As he learns this command and is doing it consistently, begin making it more challenging by turning, walking fast, walking slow, and going different directions.

At this point in the training, with this method, always start with the "Let's go!" command and tell your Pug to heel as he arrives at your left side and you begin walking forward together.

After a week or two of this training, or when your Pug seems to understand what you want him to do, begin by having your Pug sit by your left side. Have some treats in your right hand, show him a treat, and tell him, "Sweetie, watch me!" When he's paying attention to you, tell him, "Sweetie, heel!" and walk forward. If he pulls ahead, tell him, "Acckk! No pull!" When he slows down, backs off the pulling, and looks back to you, praise him and repeat the watch me command. When he watches you, praise him enthusiastically.

This requires a little more concentration, so be sure you keep the sessions short and upbeat, and praise your Pug's successes.

When you take your Pug for a walk, don't ask him to heel the entire way. Instead, go back and forth between the let's go and the heel. Offer some variety and some challenge. However, once you start this training, don't let your Pug pull on the leash. Whenever he's on the leash, he is to respect it and never, ever pull on it.

Tips for Successful Training

Your training will only be successful if you practice it regularly and use the training commands throughout your day. If the training is confined only to training sessions, your Pug will think it applies only to those sessions. I've supplied many examples of how you can use these commands, but find your own, too. After all, my daily routine is not the same as yours, so we'll use the commands differently.

Your Pug should not be allowed to pull on the leash when you're walking.

Here are a few other tips to help your training be successful:

- Your Pug is a member of your family, but remember, he is a dog and not a person in a fuzzy Pug suit. He has different instincts and thought processes than you do and will react differently.

- If he makes a mistake, don't take it as a personal affront. It was just a mistake.

- Limit your Pug's freedom; he shouldn't be off leash outside a fenced area until he's 2 to 3 years old and well trained.

- Teach your Pug that his name and the word "Good!" are magic words. He should look at you and wag his little curly tail when he hears those words.

- Timing is everything. Praise him, "Good boy!" as he does something right (not later) and interrupt him, "Acckk!" as he makes a mistake (not afterward).

- Keep your training fun!

Keep your training sessions short, positive, and fun.

The Least You Need to Know

🏠 Teach your Pug the eight basic obedience commands—"Sit," "Release," "Lie down," " Stay," "Come," "Watch me," "Let's go," and "Heel."

🏠 The basic commands are the foundation for everything you will ever teach your Pug in the future.

🏠 Keep your training session fun, upbeat, but under control.

🏠 Use these commands everywhere, not just in training.

Chapter 16

Pugs Will Make Mistakes

In This Chapter

- 🏠 Is your Pug a troublemaker?
- 🏠 Are you causing your Pug's problem?
- 🏠 Finding problems and solutions
- 🏠 Looking at some other behavior problems

Being cute has its advantages, and don't think Pugs don't know they're adorable—they do! Those big, dark, deerlike eyes can look so innocent, even when your Pug is standing in the midst of the trash from the kitchen trash can.

Most Pugs don't intend to get into trouble. For the most part, they do want to be good dogs. Unlike some other dogs and breeds, they don't deliberately try to make you angry, but sometimes things just happen. Perhaps a scent in the kitchen trash was too appealing or the open front door and the neighbor's cat were just too much to resist.

Pugs can get into trouble. Let's take a look at why Pugs do what they do, and what you can do to change things.

Why Do Pugs Get Into Trouble?

Your Pug dumped over the kitchen trash can initially because something in it—that tuna fish can or a meat wrapper—was just too appealing. Then, when the can tipped over and everything fell out, your Pug found that it was full of treasures—wrappers, empty cans, and other bits of food—and his behavior promptly became self-rewarding. He didn't need any rewards from you (praise or treats), because his bad behavior was rewarded by the treasures he found in the trash can.

When you're looking at problem behaviors, keep in mind that these behaviors are not problems to the dog. Your Pug does things for a reason. You might not be aware of the reason, or you might not agree with him, but he knows exactly what he's doing!

Reward isn't the only reason Pugs act up. Other things can affect problem behavior—sometimes quite significantly.

Is Your Pug Healthy?

Poor health or changes in health can trigger changes in behavior. A urinary tract infection or incontinence can cause housetraining accidents. Puppy teething or an infected tooth can cause a dog to chew on inappropriate things, mouth your hands, or act grumpy. If your Pug has an abrupt change in behavior, schedule a visit to your veterinarian. Tell your vet what has happened and that you want to be sure a health problem isn't behind the misbehavior. If your dog gets a clean bill of health, then you can look at it from a behavioral viewpoint.

Many dog owners assume any behavior problem is rooted in "bad" behavior, but most experts feel that at least 20 percent of all behavior problems have a health-related issue behind them. That's 2 dogs out of 10—a significant number. That's why it's so important to see your vet first, before beginning any *behavior modification* or training. It would be very unfair to punish your dog for behavior caused by a health problem, behavior he can't control.

Pug Speak

Behavior modification is the process of changing behavior. It combines training with an understanding of why dogs do things, and changing the dog, the owner, and the environment so the dog no longer needs to do that behavior.

What Does Your Pug Eat?

Most Pugs will thrive on just about any good-quality food. By "good-quality food," I mean exactly that—a food that's not cheap, generic, or lesser-quality (see Chapter 10).

However, some dog foods high in cereal grain carbohydrates are known to cause a type of hyperactivity in some dogs—including Pugs. Dogs affected by this can't hold still and are much more active than normal.

If you suspect a food-related problem, read the label of the food you are feeding. Most Pugs do very well on a dry kibble food that's about 26 to 28 percent protein and 8 to 10 percent fat. The carbohydrates should be from roots, tubers, and fruits, not from cereal grains. Feed a food that doesn't contain a lot of sugar and artificial preservatives, colorings, and additives.

Pug Smarts

If you do switch foods, take your time. Add a little new food to the old, and gradually—over 2 to 3 weeks—add more of the new food (see Chapter 10).

Is Your Pug a Lap Dog?

Of course your Pug is a lap dog—that's why you got a Pug!
However, don't forget that Pugs are still dogs; they're not stuffed
toys or ceramic statues. Your Pug needs daily exercise to keep his
body strong. He needs playtime so he can have fun with you, so you
can enjoy each other. Your Pug also needs to train with you and
learn new things so his mind stays active and sharp.

There's nothing wrong with your Pug spending time on your lap
or snoozing right next to you. But be sure he doesn't spend *all* his
time on your lap. Of course, that's
not good for you, either. We all
need to get up, move around, exercise, play, laugh, and learn new
things. When your Pug doesn't get
enough exercise, he's going to look
for things to do, and that might be
chewing on your shoes or furniture, barking at your neighbors, or
digging up the backyard.

Bet You Didn't Know

The amount of exercise
a dog needs will vary
from dog to dog. A nice 4- to
5-block walk around the neighborhood would be enough for
a Pug puppy, but a 3-mile
walk would be better for a full-
grown, healthy adult Pug.

Your Pug Needs Stuff to Do

A bored Pug is going to find something to do to amuse himself, and
you probably won't like what he chooses to do. Do something with
him every day to keep his mind active and sharp; this will, in turn,
help alleviate his boredom:

- Play games with your Pug that make him use his mind. Teach
  him the names of family members and then play hide-and-seek.
  "Where's Mom? Go find Mom!"

- Teach him the names of his toys and then have him pick out
  that toy from a group of his toys. "Find the ball!"

- Teach your Pug some tricks. Shake paws is fun, but more elaborate tricks are even more fun. Weave between your legs, bow, say your prayers, or counting are a few that aren't hard to teach.

- Practice his obedience training regularly, and continue to teach him new intermediate and advanced commands either at a dog training club or on your own. Teach him to heel, stay, come off leash, and obey hand signals (instead of verbal commands).

- Get involved in a dog sport or activity so he has something else to occupy his mind and body. Pugs are wonderful therapy dogs.

- If your Pug gets into trouble when he's left alone, give him a toy before you leave—a rawhide, a biscuit, or a toy that dispenses treats as the dog plays with it.

- Let him watch the birds at a bird feeder. You might be surprised by how much your Pug enjoys watching the birds.

A bored Pug is more apt to get into trouble than one who gets a lot of exercise and attention.

Are You the Leader?

Pugs lacking leadership can develop a host of behavior problems, such as leg lifting, marking, mounting, humping, and other unacceptable behaviors. Aggressive behavior toward family members is common, as is destructive behavior around the house. Food guarding, toy guarding, and similar behaviors are also not unusual.

Watch Out!

If your Pug is an adult and thinks he's the leader and you're trying to change things, be careful. If you even think he could bite you, hire a trainer or behaviorist to help you.

In your Pug's eyes, if you aren't the leader, someone must assume the position! If you haven't yet convinced your Pug you are the leader, you need to change how he regards his—and your—position in the family hierarchy. (If you need to refresh your leadership skills, go back to Chapters 5 and 14 and re-read the information.)

What Do Pug Owners Do to Cause Problems?

As a dog obedience instructor, I watch dogs and their owners every day. I watch how the dog owners interact with their dogs, and I marvel at how well dogs get along in our world in spite of us! Unfortunately, we are often the cause of our dogs' behavior problems. And worse yet, the problems we cause are the hardest to solve because it's harder to see problems within ourselves than to see the problems in our dogs.

Understand What You're Doing

It's important to understand that everything we do with and to our dogs affects them in some way. Just like a stone tossed into a lake causes ripples to flow across the entire surface of the lake, everything we do with our dogs does something to them. Soft, friendly eye contact will give our dog pleasure, while hard, angry eye contact will cause them to flinch. A friendly ear rub will be rewarded with a tail wag, while a harsh slap will cause the dog to cower. A piece of food from our plate will teach the dog to beg.

Even our own personalities and the way we interact with our dogs can affect them. The most common type of Pug owners I see are the overpermissive owners. Overpermissive owners want to spoil their dogs and usually freely admit they do. These owners don't set enough rules, or when they do set rules, they don't enforce them. These owners are not the dog's leader, and many problem behaviors can develop.

Another type of Pug owner I see often is the overprotective owner. Overprotective owners are so concerned that something will harm their dog that they don't allow the Pug to be a dog. By overprotecting their Pug, they take away his ability to cope with the world around him.

I also see owners who are overly demanding. Demanding owners would prefer the dog to be a furry robot who follows each and every order exactly as given. Dogs, of course, will make mistakes, and these owners will never tolerate mistakes. Pugs of demanding owners will never measure up, no matter how hard they try.

Overly emotional owners are quick to get excited or quick to react and often end up with dogs just like them. Unfortunately, during episodes of excitement, these dogs—especially reactive younger dogs—can get out of hand. Luckily, most adult Pugs are calm enough to tolerate these owners without getting into too much trouble, although Pug puppies will become emotional along with their owners.

Bet You Didn't Know

Everything we do with our dogs causes a reaction of some kind in them. We must be aware of ourselves and what we do to our dogs before we can change our dogs' behavior.

Many dog owners are also very inconsistent. They demand good behavior one day and don't follow through the next day. Because the rules are inconsistently enforced, the dog's behavior is also inconsistent.

Unfortunately, it's very difficult for us to see problems within ourselves. And because most of our friends and family members don't want to cause hard feelings, very few will comment on our shortcomings. However, before we can change our dog's behavior, we have to look within ourselves and recognize what we might be doing to cause the behavior.

Remember, a good leader is not overprotective, is not over-emotional, and does not demand more than the dog can do. A good leader is loving and affectionate, calm and consistent, fair yet firm, and demands respect from the dog. What are you doing that is contrary to that?

Making Changes

Your dog can develop behavior problems for a variety of reasons. Food, exercise, boredom, your reactions to him, and your emotions can all play a part, as can his health. Your household routine and how dedicated you are toward his training also play a part in his behavior. So many different factors lead toward problem behaviors that trying to solve those problems can be challenging. However, it can be done. Let's start at the beginning:

- Be sure your Pug is healthy. Don't assume he's healthy; make an appointment with your veterinarian and tell your vet why you are there.

- Make and keep a regular daily schedule for training. Fifteen minutes of sit, lie down, stay, heel, and come—all on leash—will help keep his skills sharp and his mind attentive.

- Use your training skills and commands throughout the day. Incorporate them into your daily activities.

🏠 Continue your Pug's socialization. Be sure he meets different people, new dogs, and other animals. An isolated Pug is an unhappy Pug.

🏠 Play with your dog every single day. Don't just toss the ball absent-mindedly while you're reading the paper; instead, get down on the floor with him or go outside and play. The time spent with you is important, but so is the laughter.

🏠 Be sure your Pug gets enough exercise. A healthy Pug should be able to do a nice, 3-mile walk every day as long as the weather is not too hot or humid.

🏠 Prevent the problems from occurring when you can. Put away the trash cans, pick up the children's toys, and put away the lawn furniture cushions.

🏠 Teach your Pug an *alternative behavior*. He can't dash out the front door if he learns to sit at the door and wait for permission to go outside.

Pug Smarts

Preventing problems from occurring might mean limiting your Pug's freedom. Don't let him have free run of the house, and supervise him more closely.

Pug Speak

An **alternative behavior** is one your Pug can do and be praised for. At the same time, it prevents another behavior from happening for which he might be corrected.

You must also understand that it takes time to change problem behaviors—both yours and your Pug's. Bad habits are hard to break. Be patient with yourself and your Pug, and concentrate on being consistent.

Common Behavior Problems and Solutions

Luckily, Pugs don't have too many behavior problems. Some like to dig and can make such a mess in the yard and get their facial wrinkles full of dirt. Pug puppies can use their mouth (and teeth!) too much, but that's easily stopped. Housetraining can be a challenge, but if you follow the advice in Chapter 6, your Pug should be housetrained in no time.

But in case your Pug decides to try something new, let's take a look at a few more behavior problems.

Mouthing and Biting

Most Pug puppies mouth and bite. After all, they don't have any hands, and that's how they manipulate the world around them. The fact that Pugs, especially Pug puppies, are small seems to lessen the impact of the mouthing and biting, but many people don't seem to understand how important it is that all dogs (even Pugs) do not bite.

Pug Smarts

If your Pug tries to use his mouth on your hands or clothing during play, lift your hands out of reach as you say, "No bite!" and get up and walk away. The play session is over.

The Centers for Disease Control in Atlanta, Georgia, has declared a "dog bite epidemic," stating that more than 4 million dog bite cases are reported yearly. When you consider that these are only the bites requiring medical attention, the numbers of actual bites are probably two to three times this number.

Every dog must learn that touching teeth to skin or clothing is absolutely forbidden. Ideally, you should start teaching these lessons when your Pug is a puppy, but even older puppies and adult dogs can learn:

🏠 Be consistent. Don't allow your Pug to bite you during play and then correct him for nipping in other situations.

Don't allow your Pug to chase children. There should be no nipping at their heels or clothing. Teach the children to play quietly with the dog, and don't allow them to run and scream.

Don't allow your Pug to grab at his leash, chew on it, mouth it, or pull against it with the leash in his mouth.

 Watch Out!
If your dog bites someone, not only can your dog be confiscated and killed, but depending on where you live, you can also face a lawsuit from the victim, medical costs, criminal charges, a fine, and possibly even jail time!

You can correct mouthing and biting in several ways. None of these corrections is better or worse than the others; some are simply more usable in certain situations. No matter what method you use, don't allow your Pug to make you angry enough to loose your temper. With dogs, aggression begets aggression, so you must remain calm and collected.

 Pug Smarts
By grabbing his leash, your Pug is trying to get you to do something or allow him to go somewhere. He's trying to establish control, so don't allow it to happen.

Have a squirt bottle full of water at hand. Set the nozzle on the mist setting rather than stream; mist won't hurt your Pug's face or eyes like a hard stream will. When your Pug nips at your heels, squirt him as you tell him, "No bite!" When he backs off, praise him quietly, "Good boy." The squirt bottle works as an interruption; it won't hurt him—in fact, many Pugs like the water. The squirt of water does get your Pug's attention so you can teach him using your voice.

If you have your hands on your dog, perhaps when you're hooking up his leash, playing with him, or petting him, and he tries to

Watch Out!

It doesn't take much force to close a Pug's muzzle and keep it closed. Just push upward on his lower jaw and close his mouth while you hold his collar or scruff of the neck with the other hand. Be calm yet firm, but don't be rough.

mouth or bite you, correct him right away without hesitation. With one hand, grab his buckle collar or the scruff of his neck (as a handle), and with the other hand, simply close his mouth by pushing upward on his lower jaw. Tell him firmly, "No bite!" Don't let go until he takes a deep sigh and relaxes. If you let go and he continues to try and mouth or bite you, close his mouth again, correct him again, and wait him out.

Jumping On People

Pugs can quickly learn that jumping on people gains them attention. Unfortunately, a Pug who jumps up and then scratches on your legs for attention can hurt—those nails are strong! Don't reward the bad behavior. If your Pugs jumps on you or scratches at your legs, don't pick him up! Don't greet him or pet him. Walk away from him, turn your back on him, or otherwise ignore that bad behavior.

Then, teach your Pug to sit. This might seem very simple, but when the dog learns to sit before you pick him up or to sit for attention, including petting from you, he will sit in front of you, quivering in anticipation of petting, and have no need to jump on you. If you consistently reward him for sitting, the jumping behavior will disappear.

Bet You Didn't Know

Teaching your dog to sit instead of jumping up requires consistency in training. Everyone involved in your dog's training must be sure the dog sits. If someone is inconsistent, the dog will continue to jump up.

You'll also have to teach your dog to sit for other people. Use his leash and simply do not allow him to jump up. Have him sit first (before people greet him) and then, when he tries to jump, restrain him using the leash as you tell him, "No jump!" Make him sit, and don't allow anyone to pet him until he's sitting.

A Pug (or any dog) who sits for petting is not jumping on people.

Barking

Pugs are not normally problem barkers, but when they decide to bark, their bark is loud and can be annoying. A Pug who is allowed to continue barking can become a problem barker, and that can cause problems with neighbors.

Start correcting barking in the house when you're close. Have a squirt bottle full of water handy. When someone comes to the door, for example, and your dog barks, walk quietly to the dog, and tell him, "Quiet!" firmly but without yelling. Mist the water

Watch Out!

Don't spray a hard stream of water in your Pug's face or eyes. You want to interrupt his barking, not hurt him. A mist will do the trick.

toward him. When the water interrupts his barking, you can tell him, "Good boy to be quiet!"

If you yell at your dog to stop barking, which is most people's first reaction, you're doing the same thing he's doing—making lots of noise. To your dog, you're barking, too, so of course he isn't going to stop. He thinks you're the reinforcements!

When you quietly tell him to be quiet as you spray the water, though, he hears the command as you make it difficult for him to continue barking. Be sure you praise him for being quiet when he does stop barking. You don't want to just correct; you must also tell him what is right.

When your dog has learned what "Quiet" means, start asking him to be quiet in other situations. Whenever he starts to bark inappropriately, tell him to be quiet, and be sure you back up your command. Again, always praise him for being quiet when he does.

If your dog barks when you're not home, you might have to set up a situation so you can catch him in the act. Go through all the motions of leaving: Get dressed; pick up your purse, wallet, or briefcase; get in the car; and drive down the block. Park the car down the block and walk back to your house with the squirt bottle in hand. When your dog starts to bark, surprise him with a "Quiet!" and a squirt. If you set him up a few times, he'll quickly learn that you have much more control than he thought!

Digging

Pugs are not normally problem diggers, although quite a few have tried to catch a gopher in the backyard. Many will dig a small hole (usually in a corner or in the garden) to bury a favorite toy or bone, and some will dig a shallow hole to use as a nest. I usually recommend that owners allow these mild earth movements; they're usually not very destructive, and the dog usually keeps to the same place for a period of time.

If the digging has become annoying, however, you can control it by giving him his own spot to dig. A kid's sandbox full of dirt or potting soil works well. To show your Pug that the sandbox is his digging spot, take half a dozen dog biscuits and stick them in the dirt so they're partially covered. Invite your dog to find the biscuits and to dig here. As he finds the biscuits, completely bury a few so he has to dig for them, and in the beginning, help him dig. For the first few days, continue to bury something in this spot and invite him to find it. When he digs elsewhere, correct him and take him back to his spot. He'll learn.

Suggestions for Other Potential Problems

Pugs are smart dogs, and sometimes that's a problem. Sometimes Pugs think too much and get themselves into trouble in the process. Where as a not-so-smart dog might relax and enjoy being fenced in, a Pug might try to dig under the fence. When you live with a smart breed, you have to think quicker than they do!

Here are a few suggestions for combating some specific Pug behaviors:

- **Digging under the fence.** Bury some rocks in the holes he digs under the fence. Then try to figure out why he's digging. Be sure he's getting enough exercise, playtime, and attention from you, and don't allow the neighborhood kids to play with him through the fence—or worse yet, tease him.

- **Barking at cars, kids on inline skates, bikes, and skateboards.** Keep him on leash in the yard, and when he barks, have him sit and turn him away from the distraction. Enforce the sit and sit-stay. If he can't sit still, turn around and walk the other direction. If he doesn't walk with you, let the leash correct him. Praise him when he does walk with you.

- **Barking in the car.** Have him ride in the car in his crate. It's much safer for him that way anyway, especially when the crate

is fastened in with a seat belt. If he still barks in the crate, use the squirt bottle. Squirt him as you tell him to be quiet. Praise him when he stops barking.

During all this training, remember to keep the emphasis on the positive. Praise him when he does something right, even if you're helping him do it. Set him up to succeed, then praise him for succeeding. Good behavior will eventually turn into good habits.

The Least You Need to Know

- 🏠 Problem behaviors are not a problem to your Pug. They're very natural behaviors.

- 🏠 Problem behaviors usually happen for a reason. Try to find out why your dog is doing what he's doing.

- 🏠 Prevent problems from happening if you can, especially when you aren't there to teach him.

- 🏠 Set up your Pug to succeed (not fail), and always praise him for succeeding.

Chapter 17

Understanding Pug Behavior

In This Chapter

🏠 Understanding how Pugs sense the world

🏠 Taking a look at Pug behaviors

🏠 Recognizing the differences between boys and girls

🏠 Getting answers to common canine questions

While on a walk with your Pug, have you ever watched him stop and stare off into the distance? Did you wonder what he was seeing? Or hearing? Our Pugs see, smell, and hear the world differently than we do. If we can fathom those differences, we can understand our dogs just a little better.

How Pugs Sense the World

Pugs use many of the same senses we do: sight, smell, hearing, taste, and touch. But how those senses are used can be different (after all, we do avoid other creatures' feces while dogs do not!), and the ability to use the senses can vary.

Interestingly enough, how the senses are used can vary among breeds of dogs. Pugs, for example, are very visual, using their sense of sight much more than many other breeds. However, even the Pug's vision is not as good as a sighthound's (such as a Greyhound) when it comes to tracking moving prey. Yet the Pug's vision in a dim or dark situation (such as inside a house) is much better than a Greyhound's. Much of this difference is due to the breed's purpose. Greyhounds were bred to hunt moving prey and had to key to movement to see their prey. Pugs were bred to be companion dogs. Moving prey was not important, but being able to see well in an artificial environment such as a Tibetan monastery or a stucco house is important.

The breed's sense of smell is not as sensitive as many other dog breeds, but it's still much better than people's. Bloodhounds and German Shepherds can smell a teaspoon of salt dissolved in a hundred gallons of water; Pugs can also smell salt (which many people think is odorless). The sense of smell is still very important to the breed, and much of what your dog learns about the world is through his nose. When your Pug is staring off into space, looking at something, he's sniffing, too.

Pugs have very good hearing. Your dog can hear mice rustle in the leaves and water running through your sprinkler lines. When he barks at night, it's because he heard something that triggered his protective instincts. Those velvet ear flaps protect very sensitive ears.

Dogs' sense of taste is one sense people don't really know a lot about yet. Oh, I'm sure dog food companies have studied it, but when you think of all the stuff dogs eat (including a whole bunch of stuff not meant to be eaten), it's hard to think that this is a particularly discriminating sense.

Pugs do not have the best canine noses, but they still smell more in this world than we do.

The sense of touch in dogs is not nearly as sensitive as it is in people, but it's still quite good. Our hands and fingers are very aware of the world we come into contact with, as is most of our skin. With Pugs, the feet pads are actually more sensitive than you might assume. Dogs are very aware of the feel and temperature of the ground or floor they're walking on. Dogs who have never walked on gravel or beach sand often look at the surface as they first step on it. When a surface is slippery, dogs are quick to react.

Watch Out!
Sun-baked asphalt or concrete can burn dogs' pads, so be careful when walking on these surfaces.

Why Do Pugs Roll in Stinky Stuff?

This has puzzled canine experts for years. If a dog has such a sensitive and discriminating sense of smell, why would he roll in cow manure or the remains of a dead animal? Some experts say that some dogs simply like those scents—to them it's a canine perfume of sorts. Other experts say the behavior is rooted in antiquity and is the behavior of a predator trying to disguise his scent. I think this is one behavior that won't be understood until dogs learn to actually talk to us.

Why Do Pugs Smell Each Others' Rear Ends?

This is another behavior people don't appreciate but is very natural to dogs. Dogs have scent glands called anal glands on either side of the anus. These glands secrete a small amount of oil each time the dog has a bowel movement. This fluid is unique to each dog, so when greeting each other, dogs take a sniff. It's like a personal perfume.

Why Does My Pug Stare Off into Space?

Some Pugs like to daydream, but if you're outside when your Pug does this, I doubt he's daydreaming. He's probably using several senses and just concentrating on what those senses are telling him. He's looking, smelling, and listening all at once, most likely at something he's trying to find or that's different enough to trigger his curiosity. When he does this, stop and watch him and see if you can spot what he's concentrating on.

Pugs see very well, and better than many other breeds of dogs, but are still somewhat nearsighted (compared to people).

Pug Behaviors

Each and every established breed of dog has some recognizable characteristics. Some physical ones, like muzzle length, eye placement, coat type, and coat color, are easy to spot. Others, such as some behaviors, are known primarily to enthusiasts of the breed. Sometimes these characteristics are shared with other breeds but might be emphasized more in a particular breed. Following are some things Pugs are famous for.

Why Is My Pug So Stubborn?

Pugs are wonderful dogs, often happy, silly clowns. They can have quite a stubborn streak, too. Once a Pug sets his mind on something, you need to out-think him to make him change his mind. Use your knowledge of your dog—what does he really like or what will he be most curious about? Food? Sounds? Something moving? Or perhaps he would look at you if you made a funny noise. Then take advantage of that break in his concentration and get his attention on you rather than on what he was focused on previously.

Don't try to fight your Pug; you'll probably lose and will only make things worse. Instead, concentrate on out-thinking him. After all, people are supposed to be smarter than dogs!

Why Does My Pug Yawn During Training?

A yawn such as this is known as a calming signal. It means you were taking the training session very seriously and your Pug wanted you to back off a little. Perhaps you were trying too hard or training too long or your Pug just needed a break.

You can try the same thing with your Pug. One day when he wants to do something like play, for example, and you would rather relax, yawn widely and turn your head away from your Pug. If you do it right, he'll look at you then go lie down. You're speaking his language, and he understood.

Why Does My Pug Pant So Much?

Pugs pant when they have narrow, convoluted nasal passages. They also pant when the weather is warm and they've been moving around a lot. But many Pug owners swear their Pugs pant when they laugh. Although many canine experts say dogs don't laugh, many dog owners will argue the point. It's not hard to believe that Pugs can laugh when you see a happy Pug with wagging, curly tail and a big, wide grin, tongue out, panting away. That's a laugh if I've ever seen one!

Why Does My Dog Bow?

Most dogs, especially most young dogs, will bow when they want to play. They lower their front end to the ground and stick their hips high in the air. Their tail is usually wagging, and their head lowered, usually with their tongue hanging out. Pugs play bow, too, but of course they are cuter than other breeds when they bow. That curly tail and wide grin make their bow special.

My Pug Thinks He's a Big Dog!

The American Kennel Club (AKC) might have classified Pugs as a Toy Breed dog, but Pugs don't know that. Pugs must often be protected from themselves, as they have no fear and will often go nose to nose with bigger dogs. Unfortunately, not all bigger dogs are safe with small dogs. Keep your Pug on leash when he's around unknown dogs, and be prepared to protect him from himself and from other dogs.

Why Does My Pug Eat Grass?

Many dogs, mine included, like to eat a variety of vegetables and fruits. Although dogs are scientifically classified as meat eaters (carnivores), many dogs prefer to eat plants and meats (omnivores).

Experts used to think a dog who ate grass had worms or ate the grass to make themselves vomit. However, neither theory seems to follow true for most dogs. We don't know why dogs eat grass. Some think the grass tastes good to dogs. Some feel the dog was hungry at the moment. Other experts have absolutely no idea.

My Pug Is Good on Leash but Horrible Off Leash

If you tried to make your Pug behave without a leash before he was fully trained and mentally mature, your Pug learned you couldn't follow through and make him behave if a leash wasn't present. Although not all dogs need a leash to be good, you're going to have to go back to using a leash for quite a while, at least until your Pug learns that when you ask him to pay attention to you, he should do it.

Girls vs. Boys

For many years, experts told parents of small children that all children should be raised the same, that there was no difference between girls and boys. Dog owners can tell you there are differences, and sometimes those differences are quite pronounced!

My Male Pug Doesn't Lift His Leg

Wonderful! I love it when a male dog of mine doesn't lift his leg; there's less chance of marking behavior. This doesn't mean there's something wrong, either. In most cases, it simply means your dog hasn't felt a need to demonstrate his superiority or position in the pack. Whatever you do, don't try to teach him!

My Male Pug Marks Everything

This behavior is, unfortunately, much more common than the preceding. Many male Pugs do mark (lift their leg and urinate), and some do not restrict it to walks. If the dog is young, neutering a male leg-lifter often helps. If the dog is 5 years old or older, the marking has usually become such a habit that neutering no longer makes a big difference.

Scrub the house very, very well using a cleaner made specifically for urine. Clean the upright surfaces where the dog has peed thoroughly, and scrub and soak the carpet all the way through the pad. Limit the dog's freedom in the house. The dog should be on leash with you, and when he's not, he's outside or in his crate.

Outside in the yard or on walks, don't allow your male Pug to urinate on every upright surface. Tell him to relieve himself when you go outside. Then, when he tries to continue marking, tell him to stop and follow through by moving him away from whatever attracted him. There's nothing quite so disgusting as a dog who moves down the street and urinates on everything.

My Female Pug Humps Other Dogs

Your Pug is simply asserting herself. She's telling the other dog she's the top dog—no pun intended. This is really a dominance issue. You can tell her to cut it out and stop her, but she'll do it again until the dog she's mounting tells her to stop by spinning around, growling, and barking at her.

My Pug Mounts Anything and Everything

The male Pug who likes to pleasure himself with a variety of objects, including stuffed toys, pillows, and legs, is overdue to be neutered. Some dogs are so into their actions (because it is pleasurable and, therefore, self-rewarding) that a mere verbal interruption won't work. Try squirting the dog with cold water every time you see it.

Canine Questions

Pugs (and other dogs) are not people. Even though they've been domesticated for thousands of years and we've made them a part of our family, there are still times when we don't understand each other.

My Breeder Called My Pug "Pet Quality"

Show-quality Pugs are those who more closely fit the breed standard (the written description of the perfect Pug). *Pet-quality* Pugs are those who deviate from the standard. Sometimes the differences between show and pet Pugs are very slight. Perhaps the pet puppies' ears don't lay just right, or the tail curl is different.

By calling your Pug a pet, your breeder was not saying he was any less a good dog. She was just saying he wasn't perfect enough to show.

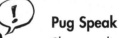

Pug Speak

Show-quality dogs compare more favorably to the breed standard than do **pet-quality** dogs.

Does One Dog Year Equal Seven Human Years?

Not really. A 1-year-old Pug is roughly the mental, physical, and sexual equivalent of a teenage human. After that, each year of your Pug's life is equal to about 5 to 7 years of human life.

My Pug's Nose Isn't Cold and Wet

A dog's nose feels cold because of the moisture that evaporates off his nose. His body temperature is actually higher than ours, so if there's no evaporation, his nose will feel warm.

Your Pug's nose should not be dry and chapped, though. If it is, take him to the vet.

Why Does My Dog Lick His Genitals?

Licking ones genitals is socially unacceptable to people, but to dogs, it's a natural behavior. He licks his genitals to keep himself clean. Cleanliness is important to continued good health.

Why Does He Bury Rawhides?

Dogs bury bones, biscuits, and rawhides to save them for later. Some dogs bury these special things in the dirt in the backyard or garden; others find other special places. One of my dogs used to bury them in my potted plants. I often found a rawhide or biscuit carefully stuffed behind an orchid or epiphyllum.

Watch Out!

If you find a treat hidden or buried outside, throw it away. Biscuits and rawhides can get moldy quickly, and that could make your Pug sick.

Some Pugs bury their treats in the house. More than one Pug owner has found biscuits hidden behind the sofa pillows or in the bed. Some Pugs go to the extreme of getting under the bed blankets and hiding the treats there.

My Pug Wants to Get Into the Cat's Litter Box

Cats evolved to eat prey, the whole prey, including the skin, small bones, and guts. Commercial cat foods include meat but also contain grains and grain products that cats often don't digest well. In addition, to make the food taste good, cat foods are high in fat. Therefore, cats pass through only partially digested food, and your Pug, smelling this, thinks this is a wonderful treat.

You're not going to stop the attraction your Pug smells in the cat litter box, so just keep the box out of your dog's reach. Put up baby gates, or keep it higher than your Pug can reach.

Why Does My Pug Want to Sleep in My Bed?

Pugs often think they're just short people and, therefore, they feel they should sleep in the big bed, too. There's no reason why your Pug can't sleep in your bedroom, but he needs to sleep in his own bed. As a puppy and up to about 2 to 3 years of age, he should be sleeping in his crate with the door closed. When he's grown up and well trained, you can take the door off the crate and let him come and go as he pleases, but continue to make him sleep there.

Dogs who share their owner's bed have a tendency to get a big head. They think they're much more important than they are. The leader or parent, you, sleeps in the big bed. Your dog sleeps in his own bed.

Pugs want to sleep on the bed with their owners, but that's not always a good idea.

Why Doesn't My Pug Pay Attention to Me?

This usually comes down to leadership. When you are your dog's leader, he will understand that you can ask him to do things, including pay attention to you. If your Pug hasn't acknowledged your leadership, he might be ignoring you on purpose.

Practice both your leadership exercises and the watch me command. Use some really good treats for the watch me, and praise your dog when he does pay attention to you.

Dogs are wonderful companions. We love them dearly, but we don't always understand them. If you look upon this as a challenge, though, to try to figure out what your Pug does and why, you'll find yourself less frustrated and more amused by the amazing creature at your side. Some people bird-watch; I dog-watch!

The Least You Need to Know

- Dogs do things for a reason. We might not understand why, but they certainly do.
- The more we know about our Pugs, the more enjoyable our time together will be.
- Dogs are fascinating creatures, and we continue to learn more about them.
- Pugs are smart, happy, and enjoyable dogs, but they can also have an amazing stubborn streak.

A Doggy Dictionary

adolescence The stage of development during which the puppy is becoming an adult and is striving for independence.

aggression A hostile reaction to stimuli. This is the fight part of the fight or flight instinct.

agility An obstacle course for dogs that can be for fun or for competition.

allergies When the body reacts to a substance that is touched, inhaled, or eaten. The body then releases histamines to fight it.

alternative behavior A behavior or action that takes the place of an unwanted behavior or action.

anaphylactic shock A potentially fatal reaction to something the body regards as foreign matter.

antibodies Disease-fighting cells that help protect a dog from coming down with a particular disease.

backyard breeder Someone who breeds dogs but has not done the research nor acquired the knowledge to do the best job possible.

behavior modification The process of changing behavior. It combines training with an understanding of why dogs do things and changing the dog, the owner, and the environment.

bitch   A female dog.

bond, bonding   The relationship between a dog and his owner that results in a strong emotional caring about each other.

breed standard   *See* standard.

buckle collar   A nylon or leather collar that fastens with some kind of a buckle. Not a slip collar.

cardiac pulmonary resuscitation (CPR)   An emergency first-aid procedure to keep the dog's heart beating and to keep breath in him.

carnivore   An animal that eats meat.

cobby   Short bodied and compact.

Come   A command that means "Run directly to me, ignoring all distractions."

conformation competition   Dog shows for evaluating a dog as compared to others of his breed and in accordance with the breed standard.

congenital health problems   Problems present at birth that might or might not be inherited.

distractions   Noises, smells, people, dogs, etc. that can break a dog's concentration.

doggy door   A door with a flap so the dog can go inside and outside at his own discretion.

double coat   A coat with two layers. One is a weather-resistant coarser outer layer, the other a softer, insulating under layer.

emergency   A potentially life-threatening injury or illness or a health threat that cannot wait until the next business day.

exercise   Physical activity or movement.

fear period   A development stage where the puppy is more apt to view things around him as frightening.

feeding trials Dog food tests in which set numbers of dogs are fed certain foods for a set period of time.

first-aid kit A container such as a tool box or tackle box containing first-aid supplies.

flea comb A comb with fine, narrow teeth that will pull fleas out of the dog's coat.

forequarters The area on a dog from his shoulders all the way down his front legs to his feet.

free feeding Leaving dog food out all day rather than having set feeding times.

genetic health problems Problems inherited from the dog's ancestors.

globular Round eyes, rather than oval or oblong.

groomer A pet professional who cares for the skin and coat of dogs.

head halter A training tool much like a horse halter. This training tool is not recommended for Pugs because of the breed's lack of a muzzle.

Heel A command that means "Walk by my left side, with your shoulder next to my leg."

herbivore An animal that eats plants.

hindquarters The area on a dog from hips down his rear legs to his feet.

housetraining The process of teaching the dog relieve himself in a specific area, to relieve himself on command, and to stop himself from going in the house.

instinct Inborn urges to respond to things in a specific manner.

interruption A verbal sound that stops unwanted behavior as it's happening.

leader To your dog, his leader is much like a parent. The leader guides the dog and sets limits. You should be your dog's leader.

Let's go A command that means "Follow me on the leash, keeping it slack, with no pulling."

Lie down A command that means "Lie down on the floor or the ground, and hold still."

markings Areas of the dog's coat of a different color than the base coat, often a contrasting color.

motivator Something your Pug likes (treats or toys) to gain his cooperation in training.

muzzle The forward part of the dog's skull from under his eyes forward to his nose, top and lower jaws, and the supporting bone.

negative attention Something negative such as scolding or a correction sought by the dog solely by misbehaving to get the owner's attention.

neuter Castration of male dogs; removal of the testicles.

omnivore An animal that eats meats and plants.

pastern The part of a dog's leg near his foot; equivalent to the human wrist.

pet quality A dog who is not of show quality as compared to the breed standard.

positive reinforcements Things the dog likes, including treats, toys, petting, and verbal praise.

praise Verbal affirmation or approval in a higher-than-normal tone of voice.

puppy mill A commercial enterprise breeding puppies for profit without regard to genetic health, individual care, or socialization.

quick The blood vessels and nerves inside a dog's toenail.

Release   A command signaling the end of an exercise.

rigid leash   A short leash fastened to a wooden dowel to make it stiff. This is a useful training tool for toy breed dogs.

shock   A life-threatening condition caused by trauma.

show quality   A dog who compares favorably to the breed standard.

single coat   A coat with only one layer; one type of coat.

Sit   A command that means "Lower your hips to the ground, keeping your front end up, and hold still."

socialization   The process of introducing a puppy to the world around him, including various people, sights, sounds, and smells.

spay   Surgically removing the female dog's ovaries and uterus.

standard   A written description of the perfect dog of the breed by looks, physical conformation, how it moves, its temperament, and its working abilities.

Stay   A command that means "Hold this particular position until you're released."

supplement   Anything added to a dog food or diet.

therapy dogs   Privately owned pets who are trained, evaluated, and certified to visit people who need some warmth and affection. Therapy dogs often visit hospitals, nursing homes, schools, etc.

training tools   Anything that's used to train the dog, including your voice, a leash, a collar, treats, or toys.

undershot   When the lower jaw protrudes so the lower teeth are in front of the upper teeth.

vaccination, vaccine   Injections that encourage the body to develop antibodies to protect against a particular disease.

Watch me   A command that means "Pay attention to me and ignore distractions."

Appendix B

Pugs on the Internet

The Internet has become a wonderful resource for everyone who has access to it. There you can find information on dogs, dog breeds (including Pugs), care, health, nutrition, dog sports, and much more. However, keep in mind that anyone can post information, and it's not always accurate. Use some common sense and be sure the information you're reading is accurate and truthful. Getting a second opinion is always good if you're not sure.

Pug Reading and Shopping

Pug Press
www.silcom.com/~pugfan
Newsletter about Pugs plus shopping.

DogWise Books
www.dogwise.com
Books and Internet forums on all canine subjects.

Esquivel and Fees Craftsmen
www.efsterling.com
Pug jewelry, including earrings, bracelets, charms, and more.

Kansas Bank Note Co.
www.kbnc.com/pdogdesigns.htm
Personal Pug-imprinted checks.

Southeast Pug Rescue and Adoption Benefit
www.rescuepug.com/shopping/shopping.html
Lots of Pug items. The proceeds benefit Pug rescue.

Pug Palace
www.pugpalace.com
Lots of different Pug items, including bobble-head Pugs.

Pug Store
www.pugstore.com
Pug calendars, note cards, and more.

Pugs Everywhere!
www.pugseverywhere.com
Pug books, art, rugs, jewelry, and more.

The Pug Zone
www.thepugzone.com
Pug shirts, jewelry, stained glass, and more.

The Prince of Dogs
www.princeofdogs.com/dog_pug
Pug statues, T-shirts, doorbells, and more.

Pug Health

American Veterinary Medical Association
www.avma.org/care4pets/
A great resource for animal health information.

NetVet Veterinary Resources
netvet.wustl.edu
Dr. Ken Boschert, Washington University, St. Louis, Missouri.
A very informative site with breaking news in the veterinary fields
and animal health, career information, and much more.

Canine Epilepsy
www.canine-epilepsy.net
Website of the Canine Epilepsy Network.

Pugs.Com
pugs.com/healthmain.htm
This is one of the best sites detailing health problems relating to Pugs. It also has links to other informative sites.

Health and Care of the Pug Dog
www.mumm.ac.be/~serge/www-pug/care
Another good resource for Pug health, including links to other health-care resources.

All Natural Remedies for Dogs and Cats
www.herb-doc.com/petcare.htm
Herbal remedies for dogs and cats as well as information about their use.

Herbs for Animals
www.herbsforanimals.com
Herbal remedies and information about their uses.

Dog Food Companies

Old Mother Hubbard
www.oldmotherhubbard.com/dogs/index.html
Wellness dog foods, treats, and nutritional information about the foods.

Canidae
www.canidae.com
Canidae Pet Foods and information about their ingredients.

Honest Kitchen
www.thehonestkitchen.com/
The Honest Kitchen dehydrated foods, ingredients, their company philosophy, and more.

California Natural

www.naturapet.com

California Natural pet products, including dog foods and the ingredients in those foods.

Natural Balance

www.naturalbalanceinc.com

Dick Van Patten's Natural Balance Pet Foods. Their meat foods come in a sausage package and make great training treats.

Solid Gold

www.solidgoldhealth.com

Solid Gold Health Products and pet foods, including dry kibble foods as well as canned.

Wysong

www.wysong.net

Wysong pet foods. Wysong is one of the first generation of better-quality foods for dogs.

Index

Y–Z